A Sentence a Day

A Sentence a Day is not your average grammar workbook. Focusing on short, playful, interesting sentences with a sense of humor, these proofreading exercises help students learn without feeling overwhelmed.

This new edition features 50 new exercises and interactive elements in its ebook+ version! Each exercise should take only a few minutes of class time, allowing for frequent, consistent reinforcement and practice of serious writing skills. Each exercise shows an incorrect sentence, a sample correction, and explanatory notes for the teacher.

With a wide range of difficulty throughout the lessons, this book is a great resource for middle school students, high school students, or anyone looking to improve their writing and grammar skills.

Samantha Prust is a writer and editor with 25+ years of experience in publishing. She has a Master of Fine Arts in Creative Writing (Fiction) from Colorado State University and is the author of the short story collection, *Romance and Other Stories*. Samantha lives with her husband and two Chihuahuas in Fort Collins, Colorado.

A Sentence a Day

Short, Playful Proofreading Exercises to Help Students Avoid Tripping Up When They Write (Grades 6–9)

Second Edition

Samantha Prust

Routledge
Taylor & Francis Group

NEW YORK AND LONDON

Designed cover image: © Getty Images

Second edition published 2025
by Routledge
605 Third Avenue, New York, NY 10158

and by Routledge
4 Park Square, Milton Park, Abingdon, Oxon, OX14 4RN

Routledge is an imprint of the Taylor & Francis Group, an informa business

© 2025 Samantha Prust

First edition published by Routledge 2007

ISBN: 978-1-032-46357-5 (pbk)
ISBN: 978-1-003-38159-4 (ebk)
ISBN: 978-1-032-78508-0 (ebk+)

DOI: 10.4324/9781003381594

Typeset in Perpetua
by Apex CoVantage, LLC

Introduction

Many teachers have adopted the daily proofreading exercises published by large companies as a way to help students practice finding and correcting errors. Sadly, many students have fallen asleep over these same exercises. I believe that these exercises try to do too much—i.e., force-feed facts and information as they also try to teach writing.

A Sentence a Day takes a different approach. It focuses on short, playful, interesting sentences with a sense of humor. Students receive proofreading practice in daily doses that don't overwhelm. Students can actually smile while they practice serious writing skills!

Each exercise should take only a few minutes of class time, allowing for frequent, consistent reinforcement. Display the exercises on your document camera projector, or simply write them on the board. Either way, I hope you will find that these exercises hold your students' attention much better than the standard fare.

—Samantha Prust

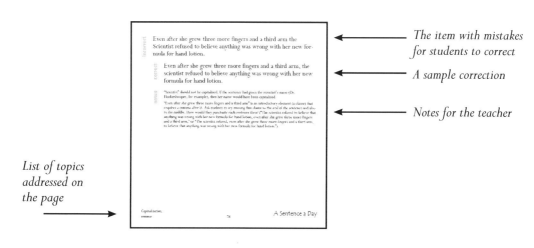

The item with mistakes for students to correct

A sample correction

Notes for the teacher

List of topics addressed on the page

The students found it incredably dificult to beleive that Mrs. Snodwhumple had ever been a teenager her self in fact they found it hard to beleive that she was human at all.

The students found it incredibly difficult to believe that Mrs. Snodwhumple had ever been a teenager herself. In fact, they found it hard to believe that she was human at all.

The correct spellings are "incredibly," "difficult," "believe," and "herself." "Believe" follows the "*i* before *e* except after *c*" rule.

The item is a run-on sentence. A period or a semicolon should be placed after "herself."

Introductory phrases like "by the way," "on the other hand," and "in fact" should be set off with commas.

A Sentence a Day

Spelling, run-ons, commas

The envilope enveloping the leter.

The envelope enveloping the letter was covered with Dr. Stinky's Scratch-n-Sniff stickers.

The item is a sentence fragment. What *about* the envelope enveloping the letter?

Try having students complete the sentence in at least two more ways—adding something before the fragment (*Bart cautiously opened the envelope enveloping the letter*) and after the fragment (*The envelope enveloping the letter was covered with Dr. Stinky's Scratch-n-Sniff stickers*).

For more practice, and some fun, challenge students to complete the fragment with other requirements as well—such as using the word "fear," including both a boy and a girl in the sentence, or adding a dog. Possibilities are endless.

"Envelope" is the correct spelling.

"Letter" has two *t*'s.

Fragments, spelling

A Sentence a Day

The nieghbors supposebly had a pet dodo bird that excaped but I no that dodo birds are extinct.

The neighbors supposedly had a pet dodo bird that escaped, but I know that dodo birds are extinct.

"Neighbors" is one of those aggravating words that does *not* follow the "*i* before *e* except after *c*" rule.

Despite how some people pronounce the word, there is no *b* in "supposedly." Similarly, there is no *x* in "escaped."

"Know" is the word needed, not "no."

The sentence is a compound sentence (two complete sentences connected with "and," "but," "or," "for," "nor," and sometimes "yet" and "so.") Therefore, it needs a comma.

A Sentence a Day

Spelling, word choice, commas

The star athlete turned out to be a alien. From the newly discovered planet gezbarkawda.

The star athlete turned out to be an alien from the newly discovered planet Gezbarkawda.

Students often create sentence fragments by putting in a period too soon. What is from the planet Gezbarkawda? This is a fragment because it doesn't have a subject or a verb. The fragment above is easily fixed by simply removing the period.

"A" is used before words beginning with a consonant sound. "An" is used before words beginning with a vowel sound.

Because "Gezbarkawda" is the name of a specific planet, it should be capitalized—even if it is fictional.

My brother, Sundar, he puts catch-up and maple sirrup on every thing.

My brother Sundar puts ketchup and maple syrup on everything.

People often use double subjects, especially when they are talking informally. Here are some examples: "My mother, she won't let me go camping with my boyfriend for three weeks in Alaska. My boyfriend, he thinks she's being unreasonable. My dad, he won't even let me talk to him about it." These double subjects are completely unnecessary. "My mother won't let me go camping" is simpler and just as clear as "My mother, she won't let me go camping."

Appositives interrupt a sentence to give more information about a noun in the sentence. Usually, they are set off with commas. However, a one-word appositive such as "Sundar" doesn't really need commas.

The correct spellings are "ketchup," "catsup," or less commonly, "catchup." It's a matter of preference, but in formal writing, use a common spelling. Other correct spellings in this item include "syrup" and "everything."

It is supposebly difficult to pat your head rub your stomach and chew gum at the same time.

It is supposedly difficult to pat your head, rub your stomach(,) and chew gum at the same time.

Although many people pronounce the word "supposebly" (with a *b*), the word is really "supposedly" (with a *d*).

Words in a series should be separated by commas. However, the final comma (the Oxford comma or the serial comma) is really optional, unless its elimination creates confusion in meaning.

Interestingly, magazine and newspaper publishers tend to leave it out, following the *Associated Press Stylebook*. Book publishers are more likely to rely on the *Chicago Manual of Style*, which recommends leaving it in. Students are often amazed to find out that authorities can differ on punctuation rules.

incorrect

Who's idea was it to allow students to ride skateboards in the hall.

correct

Whose idea was it to allow students to ride skateboards in the hall?

notes

Any sentence that asks a question should have a question mark at the end.

"Who's" is a contraction of "who is." A test: try substituting "who is" in the sentence to see if it makes sense. If it does, use "who's." If it doesn't, use "whose."

A Sentence a Day

Question marks,
word choice

A even-toed ungulate which is better known as a camel keeps the sand out of it's eyes with 3 eyelids.

An even-toed ungulate, which is better known as a camel, keeps the sand out of its eyes with three eyelids.

"An" is used before words beginning with a vowel sound.

"Which is better known as a camel" is an appositive. It interrupts the flow of the sentence to give more information about "ungulate" and should be set off with commas.

"Its" is a pronoun used to show ownership or possession. There is no apostrophe in it.

Numbers smaller than ten are generally spelled out, not written as numerals. Therefore, "3" should be written as "three."

Word choice,
commas, spelling

A Sentence a Day

After Jamal took a break to walk his Iguana and pet his Python he went back to work on his marshmellow sculpture.

After Jamal took a break to walk his iguana and pet his python, he went back to work on his marshmallow sculpture.

"After Jamal took a break to walk his iguana and pet his python" is an introductory element (a clause). Therefore, it should be followed by a comma.

"Iguana" is a kind of lizard, just as "python" is a kind of snake. But they aren't the names of *specific* iguanas or pythons. If the iguana's name is "Ethel," "Ethel" is what should be capitalized, not "iguana."

"Marshmallow" is the correct spelling.

A Sentence a Day

Commas, capitalization, spelling

The mall closed it's doors lifted into the air and flew off into space with a large and handsome truck stop.

The mall closed its doors, lifted into the air(,) and flew off into space with a large and handsome truck stop.

Never mind that the mall in this sentence is behaving in a decidedly peculiar fashion. It is doing three things, and those three things should be separated by commas. The final comma in a series is called a serial comma and is considered optional.

"It's" is a contraction of "it is." A test: substitute "it is" in the sentence to see if "it's" is what is needed. If it doesn't sound right, "its" should be used.

Pleeze do not sneeze, or wheeze near there cheeze.

Please do not sneeze or wheeze near their cheese.

Annoying as it may be that all these words with an "eez" sound aren't spelled alike at the end, they are not.

There should not be a comma before "or" because "wheeze near their cheese" is a dependent clause.

Should it be "there," "they're," or "their"? "Their" is the word used to show possession. It is "their" cheese someone should not be sneezing or wheezing near.

A Sentence a Day

Spelling, commas,
word choice

As Lionel was finally doing his laundry after letting it sit, in a heap for two weeks. He watched in horror as a mustard splotch on one of his shirts, unstuck itself and crawled out of the laundry basket, and down the hall.

As Lionel was finally doing his laundry after letting it sit in a heap for two weeks, he watched in horror as a mustard splotch on one of his shirts unstuck itself and crawled out of the laundry basket and down the hall.

Students commonly create sentence fragments simply by inserting a period too soon. Read aloud the first "sentence" so that students hear how it is left hanging and needs to be completed.

All the commas in the incorrect version are unnecessary. (An argument can be made for including one before "in a heap" for emphasis. In that case, a comma is necessary after "heap" as well.)

Some grammarians would point out that splitting the verb "was doing" with the word "finally" is not a good idea. They might leave out the word "finally" altogether or write, "As Lionel was doing his laundry, finally, he . . ." Others would leave the "finally" where it is.

"I looked over the close in my closet and decided I'm going to wear to scarfs around my neck and one on my head, to," said Hanako. "Is that *all* your going to where?" gasped her sister.

"I looked over the clothes in my closet and decided I'm going to wear two scarves around my neck and one on my head, too," said Hanako.
   "Is that *all* you're going to wear?" gasped her sister.

The corrected sentences use "to, two, and too" correctly. Although "to" and "too" have several meanings, to keep the basics straight, think "to" as in "to town," "two" as in "count to two," and "too" as in "too much ice cream."

"Clothes" refers to what you wear. "Close" is what you do to a door.

"Wear" is what you do with clothes. "Where" is used to refer to a place.

In dialogue, a new paragraph begins with each change of speakers.

A Sentence a Day

13

Word choice,
dialogue

The eye-catching float adorned with silver and yellow balloons. Carried a gigantic ice sculpture of a earthworm, the high schools mascot.

The eye-catching float adorned with silver and yellow balloons carried a gigantic ice sculpture of an earthworm, the high school's mascot.

The two sentence fragments above can be turned into a complete sentence simply by removing the period.

Since "earthworm" begins with a vowel sound, the phrase should be "an earthworm."

The mascot "belongs" to the high school. Therefore, an apostrophe is needed before the *s*.

A skunk wandered through the neighbor hood and caused quit a scene when it ambled over to the busstop and crawled up on the bench.

A skunk wandered through the neighborhood and caused quite a scene when it ambled over to the bus stop and crawled up on the bench.

"Neighborhood" is one word.

"Bus stop" is two words.

"Quite" is the word needed above, not "quit," which means to give up.

A Sentence a Day

Spelling, word choice

Iris ate icecream on the ice berg while the yak yakked about frozen Yogurt.

Iris ate ice cream on the iceberg while the yak yakked about frozen yogurt.

"Ice cream" is two words.

"Iceberg" is one word.

There is no need to capitalize "yogurt."

The scarred moose got lose and vamoosed disapearing behind the caboose.

The scared moose got loose and vamoosed, disappearing behind the caboose.

Some students may insist that the moose really was *scarred* in an accident, not *scared*. They could be right, although it is more likely that the moose is disappearing because it is scared, not because it is scarred. However, allow their argument. It's good for them to see that small things like an *r* can completely change the meaning of a sentence.

"Lose" and "loose" are often confused. "Lose" means to fail to win or to misplace, and it rhymes with "shoes." "Loose" has many meanings, including not fastened, not restrained, and others, and it both rhymes with and looks similar to "goose."

"Disappearing" needs two *p*'s.

"Disappearing behind the caboose" is an ending element (a phrase) that interrupts the flow of the sentence. It should be preceded by a comma.

A Sentence a Day

Spelling, commas

"Before you buy shoes for your pet millipede", he said. "Consider the cost.

"Before you buy shoes for your pet millipede," he said, "consider the cost."

Commas go *inside* (before) closing quotation marks.

If a quotation is interrupted with a dialogue tag ("he said," "she said," etc.), the next part of the quotation should not be capitalized unless it starts a new sentence. "Before you buy shoes for your pet millipede, consider the cost" is a complete sentence interrupted with "he said." Therefore, "consider" is not capitalized.

Quotation marks always come in pairs. One set is always followed by another.

Bram had a hard time remembering things, he always came to school with a sticky note list stuck in the middle of his fourhead.

Bram had a hard time remembering things. He always came to school with a sticky note list stuck in the middle of his forehead.

This type of run-on sentence is called a comma splice. Two complete sentences cannot be separated by a comma. Use a semicolon, a period, or a conjunction. Some conjunctions don't necessarily require a comma ("because," "if," "though," "since"). Others do require a comma, such as coordinating conjunctions ("for," "and," "nor," "but," "or," "yet," "so," or FANBOYS).

An interesting exercise is to have students see how many ways they can fix the comma splice. A few ways:

- Because Bram had a hard time remembering things, he always came to school with a sticky note list stuck in the middle of his forehead.
- Bram had a hard time remembering things. That's why he always came to school with a sticky note list stuck in the middle of his forehead.
- Bram always came to school with a sticky note list stuck in the middle of his forehead because he had a hard time remembering things.

"Forehead" is the correct spelling.

Aisha asked the telemarketer, "if she could call him back tomorow around dinnertime at his home phone number."

Aisha asked the telemarketer if she could call him back tomorrow around dinnertime at his home phone number.

Quotation marks can be compared to a "bubble" in a cartoon strip. The bubble shows the words coming out of the cartoon character's mouth. Similarly, quotation marks surround only the words a character actually says. The incorrect item above is an indirect quote. It tells what Aisha asked, but without using her exact words. The sentence could also be corrected this way: Aisha asked the telemarketer, "May I call you back tomorrow around dinnertime at your home phone number?"

"Tomorrow" has two *r*'s.

Incidentally, Aisha's technique for dealing with telemarketers can be very satisfying.

Oliver blew a fuse this morning, because his little brother fed his homework to squeezy there pet Boa Constrictor.

Oliver screamed, yelled, and cried this morning because his little brother fed his homework to Squeezy, their pet boa constrictor.

The phrase "blew a fuse" is a cliché. See if students can come up with more specific or original ways to describe being angry or upset.

"Because" is a conjunction that is not generally preceded by a comma. The conjunctions that *are* generally preceded by a comma when they separate two sentences are "for," "and," "nor," "but," "or," and sometimes "yet" and "so" (FANBOYS).

"Squeezy" is the name of a specific boa constrictor. Therefore, it is a proper noun that should be capitalized. "Boa constrictor" is the name of a type of snake, but it is not the name of a specific, individual snake. Therefore, it is *not* capitalized.

"Their" is used to show possession. It was "their" boa constrictor; it belonged to them.

A Sentence a Day

Clichés, commas, capitalization, word choice

Irregardless of what I thought of the movie I definitely enjoyed the gigantic bucket of buttered popcorn that me and my friend shared.

Regardless of what I thought of the movie, I definitely enjoyed the gigantic bucket of buttered popcorn that my friend and I shared.

Some would say that "irregardless" is not really a word, just as "ain't" is not. But both clearly *are* words, since people use them all the time. However, they are considered "nonstandard." They should not be used in most writing or speaking.

"Me and my friend" is increasingly showing up everywhere. "My friend and I" is the correct form. An interesting point of discussion is *why* "me and my friend" is becoming so common. Some say it might have to do with a growing self-centeredness in our society. That "me first" attitude seeps into language as well as behavior. It's something to think about, in any case, and could lead to an interesting discussion. (The item is not written as a direct quotation. If it had been, "irregardless" and "me and my friend" could remain in order to record the person's words accurately.)

Dont slam the door, you will wake up the wombats.

Don't slam the door because you will wake up the wombats.

"Don't" needs an apostrophe. As in all contractions, the apostrophe takes the place of the letter or letters left out in the contraction. (In this case, it stands for the *o* in "not.")

This type of run-on sentence is called a comma splice. Two complete sentences cannot be separated by a comma. Use a semicolon, a period, or a conjunction. Some conjunctions don't necessarily require a comma ("because," "if," "though," "since"). Others do require a comma, such as coordinating conjunctions ("for," "and," "nor," "but," "or," "yet," "so," or FANBOYS).

Apostrophes,
run-ons

Adriana knew something was wrong when she seen a giraffe poke it's head out of her chimney.

Adriana knew something was wrong when she saw a giraffe poke its head out of her chimney.

The correct verb form here is "saw." "Seen" always needs a helping verb before it—she *has* seen, she *will have* seen, she *was* seen, she *will be* seen, etc.

"It's" is a contraction of "it is." "Its" (without the apostrophe) is always used to show possession of some kind (its fur, its wheels, its stomach, its head, etc.).

In the allie behind the restraunt Margo was cornered by a flock of fryed chickens who demanded that she put down her cole slaw and mashed potatos and come out with her hands up.

In the alley behind the restaurant, Margo was cornered by a flock of fried chickens who demanded that she put down her coleslaw and mashed potatoes and come out with her hands up.

The introductory prepositional phrases ("in the alley behind the restaurant") should be followed by a comma. They precede the main part of the sentence: "Margo was cornered by a flock of fried chickens."

The word "potato" does not end in an *e*. An *e* is added, however, when the word is made plural. Other spelling corrections include "alley," "restaurant," "fried," and "coleslaw."

Instead of ringing the phone made a sound like boots squishing thru mud.

Instead of ringing, the phone made a sound like boots squishing through mud.

"Instead of ringing" is an introductory phrase. (It comes before the main part of the sentence: "the phone made a sound like boots squishing through mud.") Therefore, it should be followed by a comma.

You might want to talk about the increasing use of "thru" in advertising, instant messages, text messages, and many email messages. The proper spelling is still "through," but it is very likely that one day "thru" will be accepted as normal. Students need to know that language rules *do* change. For example, "skyscraper" used to be considered a slang word. Now it is actually the proper name for very tall buildings.

To get alot of attention put on a carrot costume and walk around on a pair of expecially high stilts.

To get a lot of attention, put on a carrot costume and walk around on a pair of especially high stilts.

"A lot" is two words, not one. No one writes "alittle." Why write "alot"? It doesn't make sense.

"To get a lot of attention" is an introductory element (a phrase) that should be followed by a comma.

People often mispronounce "especially" as "expecially"—which leads them to spell the word incorrectly as well. There is no *x* in "especially."

Winona didn't take the attention she got from Mateo and Jin for granite, and she kept the boy's hundreds of letters in a special file cabinet in her closet.

Winona didn't take the attention she got from Mateo and Jin for granted, and she kept the boys' hundreds of letters in a special file cabinet in her closet.

"Granted" is the word needed, not "granite," which is a kind of rock.

In most cases, the apostrophe goes after the *s* if the possessive refers to more than one person. In this case it does. (An example of when it would not is, "She shopped in the women's department.") If it referred to only one boy's letters, the apostrophe would go before the *s*.

The banana split that I ate last night at humongo ice cream shoppe, sat in my stomache like a ball of hardened clay.

The banana split that I ate last night at Humongo Ice Cream Shoppe sat in my stomach like a ball of hardened clay.

Humongo Ice Cream Shoppe is the name of a store, so it should be capitalized.

There is no need for the comma before "sat."

"Stomach" is the correct spelling.

"Shoppe" is part of the store's name, so the spelling should remain. Many retail establishments use the spelling "shoppe" to give their stores an old-fashioned flavor. (Whether their technique is effective or not is another question.)

I crept along the hallway to suprise Mom with a boquet of flours, I also wanted to shock my brother with the photo I took of him kissing his girlfriend when he was suppose to be studying at the library.

I crept along the hallway to surprise Mom with a bouquet of flowers, and I also wanted to shock my brother with the photo I took of him kissing his girlfriend when he was supposed to be studying at the library.

It takes an eagle eye to catch all the little (and big!) things wrong with this sentence. "Bouquet" and "flowers" are the correct spellings of Mom's "surprise," not "suprise."

This type of run-on sentence is called a comma splice. Two complete sentences cannot be separated by a comma. Use a semicolon, a period, or a conjunction. Some conjunctions don't necessarily require a comma ("because," "if," "though," "since"). Others do require a comma, such as coordinating conjunctions ("for," "and," "nor," "but," "or," "yet," "so," or FANBOYS).

Even though it sounds like "suppose to" when we say it, the correct spelling is "supposed to."

incorrect

Our nieghbor poured cool gray concrete over his entire yard cuz he didnt want to water the grass anymore.

correct

Our neighbor poured cool gray concrete over his entire yard because he didn't want to water the grass anymore.

notes

This item is a sea of misspelled words. "Neighbor" is, unfortunately, one of those words that breaks the "*i* before *e* except after *c*" rule.

Use "because," not "cuz." "Cuz" is used only in the most informal writing among friends.

"Didn't" needs an apostrophe. The word is a contraction of "did" and "not," and the apostrophe is used in place of the missing *o*.

My best freind sally, she says you should always wash your elbows before going out 2 eat.

My best friend Sally says you should always wash your elbows before going out to eat.

"Friend" is very commonly misspelled as "freind." The word does follow the "*i* before *e* except after *c*" rule.

There is no reason to say "my best friend Sally" *and* "she." The sentence needs only one subject.

Using "2" instead of "to" may be acceptable in text messages to friends, but it should not be used in other kinds of writing.

I should of bought the robot, it would of cleaned my room, taken out the trash, and done my homework.

I should have bought the robot. It would have cleaned my room, taken out the trash(,) and done my homework.

When we speak, the contractions "should've" and "would've" sound like "should of" and "would of." The "of" should be "have," however. (The item could also be written like this: I should've bought the robot. It would've cleaned my room, taken out the trash, and done my homework.)

This type of run-on sentence is called a comma splice. Two complete sentences cannot be separated by a comma. Use a semicolon, a period, or a conjunction. Some conjunctions don't necessarily require a comma ("because," "if," "though," "since"). Others do require a comma, such as coordinating conjunctions ("for," "and," "nor," "but," "or," "yet," "so," or FANBOYS).

"Your such a know-it-all" said the Heart, to the Brain.

"You're such a know-it-all," said the heart to the brain.

"You're" is a contraction of "you are" and is the word needed in this sentence.

The quotation should be separated from "said the heart to the brain" with a comma.

There is no need for a comma after "heart."

There is no need to capitalize "heart" and "brain."

"Your overly sensitive", said the brain. To the heart.

"You're overly sensitive," said the brain to the heart.

This short item has a lot wrong with it. First, "your" should be "you're." "You're" is a contraction of "you are."

The comma should go inside (before) the closing quotation marks. Except in very rare cases, the comma *always* goes inside the quotation marks.

Finally, "To the heart" is a sentence fragment. It is really part of the previous sentence.

Her and me are gonna go shoping for a Collie puppy and a yo-yo.

She and I are going to go shopping for a collie puppy and a yo-yo.

Ask students what they would say if only one person were going shopping. Would they say, "Her is going shopping"? "Me is going shopping"? Of course not. Then why say "her and me"?

"Gonna" should be "going to."

"Shopping" needs two *p*'s. It is common to double the final consonant before adding "ing."

"Collie" is the name of a kind of dog, but it is not the name of a specific dog, like "Sophie" or "Spot." Therefore, it should not be capitalized.

"Alright, I'll do it" sighed the dragon. "I'am not going to like it, but I'll stop breatheing fire on the village."

"All right, I'll do it," sighed the dragon. "I'm not going to like it, but I'll stop breathing fire on the village."

"All right" is two words.

"All right, I'll do it" should be set off from "sighed the dragon" with a comma.

"I'am" is a common misspelling, even though it doesn't make much sense. An apostrophe in a contraction stands for a letter left out, but in "I'am," nothing is left out. "I'm" is the correct spelling.

"Breathe" has an *e* at the end. "Breathing" does not. In most cases, the final *e* is dropped before adding "ing" to a word that ends in *e*.

If you happen to have a dragon, it's nice to have an agreeable one.

A Sentence a Day

Spelling,
commas

He held out his hands to catch the football and then he glanced at Kiyoko to see if she was chearing for him and when he turned back the football hit him right in the face.

He held out his hands to catch the football and then glanced at Kiyoko to see if she was cheering for him. When he turned back, the football hit him right in the face.

"Cheering" is the correct spelling.

The item is one long run-on sentence. You might have students experiment to see how many ways they can rewrite the sentence, correcting it and keeping the same meaning. Two examples:

After holding out his hands to catch the football, he glanced at Kiyoko to see if she was cheering for him. When he turned back, the football hit him right in the face.

He held out his hands to catch the football. He glanced at Kiyoko to see if she was cheering for him. He turned back. The football hit him right in the face.

"You hafta let me go mom," whined Keisha. "I want to see the singing burro"!

"You have to let me go, Mom," whined Keisha. "I want to see the singing burro!"

"Hafta" should be "have to."

Because "Mom" is what Keisha calls her mother, it is a name that should be capitalized.

Because Keisha is directly addressing her mother, "Mom" should be set off with commas.

The exclamation point belongs inside the quotation marks since it applies to the sentence, "I want to see the singing burro!"

A Sentence a Day

Spelling, capitalization, commas,
quotation marks

After the tiny baby bird opened it's tiny beak, and let out an ear-splitting squawk that made my sister drop her Slurpee. I laughed.

After the tiny baby bird opened its tiny beak and let out an earsplitting squawk that made my sister drop her Slurpee, I laughed.

"Its" (with no apostrophe) is the word needed to show possession. (The beak "belongs" to the baby bird.)

The item is really one sentence. "I laughed" is the main part of the sentence (the independent clause). "After the tiny baby bird opened its tiny beak and let out an earsplitting squawk that made my sister drop her Slurpee" is a very long introductory element (a subordinate clause).

Word choice,
fragments

A Sentence a Day

I ain't gonna be no candy cane in no school play!

I'm not going to be a candy cane in any school play!

The incorrect version of this sentence has a certain flavor missing in the correct version. You might want to see if students have any ideas why the correction is less satisfying than the original.

"Ain't" is indeed a word. It is used all the time, but it's considered "nonstandard" usage and should be avoided in most circumstances.

"Gonna" should be "going to."

A very old guideline in English is to avoid double negatives. Since the sentence starts out early on with a "not," the "no's" should be omitted.

Than the career counselor goes, "we have alot of job openings for accountants that are abominable snowmen.

Then the career counselor said, "We have a lot of job openings for accountants who are abominable snowmen."

"Then" is the correct word in this sentence because it refers to time/order. "Then" also means "in that case," "as a necessary consequence," "besides," and some other similar things. "Than" is used when comparing things. "Upon arrival, I knew I had a better costume than anyone else at the party, and then I won the costume contest."

The career counselor didn't "go." She "said." Informally, people use "go" instead of "said" a lot, but it's better to avoid it, especially in writing.

"A lot" is two words.

The first word in a sentence should be capitalized. The first word in the sentence the career counselor is saying should therefore be capitalized.

Quotation marks always come in pairs. They should appear at the beginning *and* the end of the quotation.

"Who" is for people. "That" is for things.

I never before new a gnu, said the new zoo worker.

"I never before knew a gnu," said the new zoo worker.

"New" is used for things that are not old. "Knew" is used for things you understand or are acquainted with.

Quotation marks go around the exact words that someone speaks.

A Sentence a Day

Word choice,
quotation marks

There is a word for every thing, including the pale area shaped like a half-moon at the base of a finger nail, its a *lunule*.

There is a word for everything, including the pale area shaped like a half-moon at the base of a fingernail. It's a *lunule*.

"Everything" is one word. So is "fingernail."

"It's" is a contraction of "it is." "Its" (without the apostrophe) is always used to show possession of some kind (its fur, its wheels, its stomach, its head, etc.).

This type of run-on sentence is called a comma splice. Two complete sentences cannot be separated by a comma. Use a semicolon, a period, or a conjunction. Some conjunctions don't necessarily require a comma ("because," "if," "though," "since"). Others do require a comma, such as coordinating conjunctions ("for," "and," "nor," "but," "or," "yet," "so," or FANBOYS).

Carmen my friend who loves music even more then chocolate had a iPod surgically inplanted in her brain.

Carmen, my friend who loves music even more than chocolate, had an iPod surgically implanted in her brain.

"Than" is the correct word in this sentence because it refers to a comparison between music and chocolate. "Then" refers to time/order or means "in that case," "as a necessary consequence," "besides," and some other similar things. "Upon arrival, I knew I had a better costume than anyone else at the party, and then I won the costume contest."

"My friend who loves music even more than chocolate" is an appositive that gives more information about the noun, Carmen. It interrupts the flow of the sentence and should be set off with commas.

What do you do with the word "iPod"? It's annoying to have a brand name that does *not* follow the rules about capitalizing proper nouns. In this case, the company has chosen to write the name of a product with a lowercase *i*. Therefore, that's the way we should write it, too. (The exception would be if "iPod" comes at the beginning of the sentence. Then it should be capitalized.)

Because it begins with a vowel sound, it should be "an iPod," not "a iPod."

The word is "implanted," not "inplanted."

A Sentence a Day

Commas, capitalization, word choice, spelling

If I had one wish. I would wish that I had a milion more wishes.

If I had one wish, I would wish that I had a million more wishes.

"If I had one wish" is a sentence fragment. Replacing the period with a comma easily fixes it, making "If I had one wish" an introductory clause.

"Million" is the correct spelling.

Be careful not to mispell your name on the entry form for the Spelling Bee.

Be careful not to misspell your name on the entry form for the spelling bee.

"Misspell" is, sadly, often misspelled. Note that the letter *s* appears twice.

There is no need to capitalize "spelling bee," just as there is no need to capitalize "the track meet" or "the club meeting." If the official name were mentioned, the name *would* be capitalized (example: Roberts County Annual Spelling Bee).

The affects of my sun burn—peeling itching blistered skin and a lot of pain—effected my ability to attend the annual beach BBQ.

The effects of my sunburn—peeling, itching, blistered skin(,) and a lot of pain—affected my ability to attend the annual beach barbecue.

Students have to be really on their toes for this one. "Effects" is a noun. "Affects" is a verb. Therefore, the sentence should read, "The effects of my sunburn . . ." and ". . . affected my ability to attend . . ."

"Peeling, itching, blistered skin, and a lot of pain" is a series that requires commas.

"Sunburn" is one word.

"BBQ" is fine for informal email or text messages. However, for most other situations, the word should be spelled out as "barbecue" or "barbeque."

Who says men are'nt nurturing, a male Emperor Penguin protects his egg for sixty days or more, and doesn't eat during the time he is waiting for the egg to hatch.

Who says men aren't nurturing? A male emperor penguin protects his egg for sixty days or more and doesn't eat during the time he is waiting for the egg to hatch.

The item above has a host of problems. First, it is a comma splice, a type of run-on sentence. "Who says men aren't nurturing?" is a question and should have a question mark.

The apostrophe is in the wrong place in "aren't."

The term "emperor penguin" describes a kind of penguin. It should not be capitalized. (If we were talking about a penguin named Frank, "Frank" *would* be capitalized.)

In most cases, a comma is not needed between the subject and the predicate of a sentence. There is no need for a comma after "more."

A Sentence a Day

Run-ons, apostrophes, capitalization, commas

The principle's principle principal is, "Treat others the way you want to be treated.

The principal's principal principle is, "Treat others the way you want to be treated."

"Principal" and "principle" are easily confused. When referring to a person, "principal" is the word. (Think, "The princiPAL is my PAL.") "Principal" is also used to mean "main, first, or foremost in importance," as in "the principal focus of the meeting." "Principle" is used to refer to a rule or standard.

If students point out that the sentence is confusing even when the words are spelled correctly, great. It is. Have them suggest ways to improve it, as in, "The principal has one main rule for students to remember: Treat others the way you want to be treated."

The sentence should end with quotation marks, as quotation marks come in pairs.

Between you and I, I'm glad the cats' stole the fish sticks.

Between you and me, I'm glad the cats stole the fish sticks.

Though many believe "between you and I" is correct, it is not. The phrase requires the objective case of the pronoun—"me." (If you don't want to try to explain this to kids having a hard time just recognizing a complete sentence, no one will blame you.)

Something you definitely *should* note is the superfluous apostrophe in "cats." After they start studying apostrophes, students all too often start sprinkling them everywhere, even where they are not needed.

A Sentence a Day

Pronouns,
apostrophes

All of the sudden the Loch Ness Monster decided to come out of the water and open a Chuck E. Cheese franchise.

All of a sudden, the Loch Ness monster decided to come out of the water and open a Chuck E. Cheese franchise.

For some unknown reason, some people say "all of *the* sudden" instead of "all of *a* sudden." Why? Who knows? The conventional phrase, and the one that should appear in written works, is "all of a sudden."

"Loch" and "Ness" are capitalized because it is the name of a lake (Lake Ness). There is no reason to capitalize "monster."

"All of a sudden" is an introductory element (a phrase) that should be followed by a comma.

Maria ceretainly can throw that javellin good.

Maria certainly can throw that javelin well.

"Well" is used to describe how someone *does* something. "Good" is used to describe a noun. Examples:

He coached them well.

He was a good coach.

She cooks well.

She is a good cook.

Have students come up with other examples of "good" and "well" being used correctly.

"Certainly" and "javelin" are the correct spellings.

A Sentence a Day

Word choice,
spelling

These ones are diferent from those ones.

These are different from those.

An oddity that has crept into our language is the use of "these ones." There is no need for the "ones." Why not just say "these"? Or "those"?

"Different" has two f's.

I ain't got no problem attending english class but I wish the teacher would stop talking to us about using good grammer. I don't want no part of learning how to speak good.

I don't have any problem attending English class, but I wish the teacher would stop talking to us about using good grammar. I don't want any part of learning how to speak well.

One thing to point out about the word "ain't" is how often it is used by writers to help suggest that a character is uneducated or not very bright. "Ain't" users can, of course, be both educated *and* bright, but others may not always perceive them that way.

"I ain't got no" is a double negative—another no-no (pun intended!).

"English" is capitalized because it is the name of a language.

"Grammar" is spelled "gramm*ar*," not "gramm*er*." Many people are surprised to learn that.

"Well" is used to describe how someone *does* something. "Good" is used to describe a noun. (It was a *good* concert. She sang *well*.)

A Sentence a Day

Word choice, double negatives, capitalization, spelling

My Mom, went to the store too buy some bread!!!!! And I ate it!!!!!

My mom went to the store to buy some bread, and I ate it.

"Mom," "dad," "grandma," "grandpa," etc., are not capitalized when they are preceded by a pronoun such as "your" or "my." However, if "Mom" is used as a person's name, it is capitalized. (Example: I looked around and saw Mom.)

"To" is the word to use, not "too." "Too" is used to express a degree of something, as in "too much ice cream." "Too" can also be used to mean "also."

Exclamation points should be used *very* sparingly. They should be reserved for the truly amazing. Eating bread doesn't qualify.

Richard didn't understand why he didn't get the job at the Insurance company. After all he was friendly in his interview and called the President "dude."

Richard didn't understand why he didn't get the job at the insurance company. After all, he was friendly in his interview and called the president "dude."

No capital letter is needed for "insurance company" since the name of the insurance company isn't used.

"After all" is an introductory expression like "on the other hand" or "nevertheless." Therefore, it needs a comma.

In most cases, "president" is not capitalized unless it is used with the president's name, as in "President Kennedy." Many textbooks teach that "President" should be capitalized when it is used to refer to the president of the United States, whether it is used with his or her name or not. However, many other references take the opposite approach—for example, the *Associated Press Stylebook* and the *Chicago Manual of Style*.

The narly not on the old tree, looked like a nome's nuckle.

The gnarly knot on the old tree looked like a gnome's knuckle.

Students may have trouble figuring out what the item above means. If they do, it's a good opportunity to point out why spelling matters. The item includes words that use "gn" and "kn" for the "n" sound.

There is no need for the comma in the sentence.

Because the meatball rolled off the table on to the floor and out the door yesterday at noon in the cafeteria.

Because the meatball rolled off the table, onto the floor(,) and out the door yesterday at noon in the cafeteria, I didn't get any protein for lunch.

Sentence fragments are not necessarily short. The fragment above is an example of a fairly long one. It needs to be completed. First have students try and make the fragment even longer, while keeping it a fragment. For example, they might write, "Because the meatball rolled off the table, onto the floor, and out the door yesterday at lunchtime in the cafeteria during the third lunch period at Hamilton Junior High in South Dakota." That long introductory element (a clause) would still be a fragment.

Items in a series need to be separated by commas. The last comma is optional.

A Sentence a Day

Fragments,
commas

Over the course of six weeks we learned how to befriend Bears, and throw a elegant holiday dinner party for eight.

Over the course of six weeks, we learned how to befriend bears and throw an elegant holiday dinner party for eight.

"Over the course of six weeks" is an introductory element consisting of two prepositional phrases. It should be followed by a comma.

There is no need to capitalize the common noun "bears."

"An" is used before words that begin with a vowel sound.

There is no need for a comma after "bears."

When pennsylvania state university honored ralph for his dedication to studing insects, he was thrilled and celebrated by giving cake crumbs to all the bugs in his lab.

When Pennsylvania State University honored Ralph for his dedication to studying insects, he was thrilled and celebrated by giving cake crumbs to all the bugs in his lab.

Names of specific schools are always capitalized, as are names of people.

"Studying" is a word that is often misspelled. The *y* is important.

A Sentence a Day

Capitalization, spelling

My dad couldn't decide weather or not to let me borrow his car again, even though I done it last week and didn't have any problems except for crashing into the tour bus outside the Museum.

My dad couldn't decide whether or not to let me borrow his car again, even though I did it last week and didn't have any problems, except for crashing into the tour bus outside the museum.

"Weather" refers to rain, sunny skies, snow, hurricanes, etc. "Whether" is the word needed for "whether or not."

"I done" is always incorrect. "Done" needs a helping verb. ("I *have* done," "I *will have* done," "We *are* done," for example.) "I did" is correct in the sentence above.

"Museum" should not be capitalized unless it is part of the name of the museum, as in "Metropolitan Museum of Art."

Fern felt kinda funny after the all-you-can-eat banana split buffet the one held every saturday night at Deserts R Us.

Fern felt kind of funny after the all-you-can-eat banana split buffet, the one held every Saturday night at Desserts R Us.

"Kinda" may be okay for very informal emails between friends. In other cases, it should be spelled "kind of."

The sentence ends with an appositive, "the one held every Saturday night at Desserts R Us." It interrupts the sentence to give us more information about the buffet. It should be preceded by a comma.

Days of the week are capitalized.

This restaurant serves "desserts," not "deserts."

"Desserts R Us" is an unfortunate name for a restaurant, and that *R* instead of "Are" is annoying. But if a restaurant chooses to spell its name that way, we have to live with it.

A Sentence a Day

Spelling, commas, capitalization

Mr. washburns old car would'nt be able to win a race against a Cheetah, which can run as fast as 70 miles per hour. Niether would Mr. washburn.

Mr. Washburn's old car wouldn't be able to win a race against a cheetah, which can run as fast as 70 miles per hour. Neither would Mr. Washburn.

"Washburn's" must be capitalized because it is a name. It also needs an apostrophe to show possession.

The apostrophe in "wouldn't" is in the wrong place.

"Cheetah" does not need to be capitalized, as it doesn't name a specific cheetah.

"Neither" is another exception to the "*i* before *e* except after *c*" rule.

I was like too tired to like wash the dishes and vacume and like do the rest of the chores my mom told me she would like me to do, so I went to the mall and like walked around and stuff with my friends.

I was too tired to wash the dishes and vacuum and do the rest of the chores my mom told me she would like me to do, so I went to the mall and walked around and talked with my friends.

The only "like" necessary in the item above is the one in "she would *like* me to do." The others are just filler words common in informal speech today.

"Vacuum" surprises many with its two *u*'s. There is no *e* at the end.

What does "and stuff" mean? A person should write what he or she means by "and stuff."

A Sentence a Day

Unnecessary words, spelling, word choice

Jeremy kinda sorta liked playing football, baking cheesecake, ect.

Jeremy kind of liked playing football and baking cheesecake.

"Kinda" and "sorta" stand for "kind of" and "sort of." Either "kind of" or "sort of" should be used here, not both phrases.

"Etc." is spelled with the *t* first—something that surprises many people, particularly those who incorrectly pronounce the word as "*eck* cetera."

"Etc." stands for "and so forth" and is used when the reader can guess what the "and so forth" might stand for. It generally follows a list of at least three items, so that a person can determine a pattern. What on earth can the "etc." stand for after "playing football, baking cheesecake"? The kind of sentence where "etc." *would* be appropriate is this one: Jeremy kind of liked playing football, soccer, basketball, etc. There we can detect a pattern—that Jeremy likes active sports.

Spelling, unnecessary words

A Sentence a Day

Even a busted clock, is right twice a day.

Even a broken clock is right twice a day.

"Broken" should be used instead of "busted" for all but the most informal conversation among friends. There is no need to place a comma between the subject and the verb of a sentence.

A Sentence a Day

Word choice,
commas

Only one mammel can fly with out the help of technology, the bat.

Only one mammal can fly without the help of technology: the bat.

"Mammal" ends in "al," not "el."

"Without" is one word, not two.

The sentence makes an announcement, a "Ta-da!" kind of announcement that means, "Note what follows." A colon or a dash is appropriate in such a sentence. A comma is not.

incorrect

"I'm not picky" Argued Alvah. "I'm particular. Nothing I eat on thursday can be green.

correct

"I'm not picky," argued Alvah. "I'm particular. Nothing I eat on Thursday can be green."

notes

A punctuation mark must separate a quotation from a dialogue tag like "argued Alvah." Generally, that punctuation mark is a comma, though sometimes an exclamation point or question mark is appropriate.

"Thursday" is a proper noun that must begin with a capital letter.

Quotation marks come in pairs. They belong at the beginning *and* at the end of a quotation. The item above lacks one at the end.

A Sentence a Day

Dialogue, capitalization, quotation marks

At the present time dan is training grass hoppers to jump over hurdles he hopes he can sell them someday to a Circus.

Dan is training grasshoppers to jump over hurdles; he hopes he can sell them someday to a circus.

"At the present time" isn't really wrong. However, there is no need for these rather formal sounding words—particularly in a sentence about grasshoppers—when the words "is training" already indicate that he is doing it at the present time, i.e., "now."

Dan is someone's name, so it should be capitalized.

Dan may be hoping to sell the grasshoppers to a circus, but he doesn't name which one. Therefore, "circus" should not be capitalized.

"Grasshoppers" is one word, not two.

Finally, the item is a run-on sentence. A period, semicolon, or conjunction is needed between "hurdles" and "he."

Talitha likes puppys and stuff.

Talitha likes puppies, kittens, bunnies, and other cute baby animals.

"Puppies" is the correct spelling.

"And stuff" is not clear. We can only guess what Talitha likes. Does she like walking puppies? Playing with them? Toilet training them? Does she like puppies and all other animals? "And stuff" needs clarification.

Spelling,
word choice

All of the sudden captain skelly exclaimed weve been hit. were sinking. I want my mommy.

All of a sudden, Captain Skelly exclaimed, "We've been hit! We're sinking! I want my mommy!"

The correct phrase is "all of *a* sudden."

"Captain Skelly" is a proper name and should be capitalized.

Since the captain is exclaiming (with good reason), his words should have exclamation points after them. His words also need to be enclosed with quotation marks.

"We've" and "we're" need apostrophes. "We've" stands for "we have," and "we're" stands for "we are."

When mr. martinez saw keith pretending to be a manekin at the mall, he goes, "didn't you miss school today because you were severely ill"?

When Mr. Martinez saw Keith pretending to be a mannequin at the mall, he said, "Didn't you miss school today because you were severely ill?"

"Mr. Martinez" and "Keith" should be capitalized because they are names. "Didn't" should be capitalized because it is the first word in the sentence that Mr. Martinez speaks.

"Mannequin" is the correct spelling.

Mr. Martinez "said." He didn't "go."

When the sentence being quoted is a question, the question mark goes *before* the quotation marks.

A Sentence a Day

Capitalization, word choice, quotation marks

"Shannon please bring in the accordions ukuleles and kazoos" said the Music teacher.

"Shannon, please bring in the accordions, ukuleles(,) and kazoos," said the music teacher.

When a person is being directly addressed, his or her name is set off with a comma. Have students try putting Shannon's name in different parts of the sentence. ("Please bring in the accordions, ukuleles, and kazoos, Shannon," or "Please bring in the accordions, Shannon, and also the ukuleles and kazoos.")

No capital is needed for "music." School subjects are *not* capitalized unless they are languages or the names of specific sections, such as "Music 101."

Items in a series should be separated by commas. The final comma is considered optional.

A comma must separate the direct quotation from the dialogue tag, "said the music teacher."

Searching for Chuck our pet chinchilla we looked everywhere even in the toilet Chuck liked to do the backstroke and in the refrigerator vegetable drawer Chuck liked to munch on radishes.

Searching for Chuck, our pet chinchilla, we looked everywhere, even in the toilet (Chuck liked to do the backstroke) and in the refrigerator vegetable drawer (Chuck liked to munch on radishes).

This proofreading item will really challenge students. It introduces parenthetical information that should be enclosed in parentheses. (Some might choose dashes, which are also acceptable.) "Chuck liked to do the backstroke" and "Chuck liked to munch on radishes" are both asides that give more information. Because they are complete sentences, they must be separated from the main part of the sentence with something more than commas.

"Our pet chinchilla" is an appositive that interrupts the sentence to give more information about Chuck. It should be set off with commas.

A Sentence a Day

Commas, parentheses

Even after she grew three more fingers and a third arm the Scientist refused to believe anything was wrong with her new formula for hand lotion.

Even after she grew three more fingers and a third arm, the scientist refused to believe anything was wrong with her new formula for hand lotion.

"Scientist" should not be capitalized. If the sentence had given the scientist's name (Dr. Hockenhooper, for example), then her name would have been capitalized.

"Even after she grew three more fingers and a third arm" is an introductory element (a clause) that requires a comma after it. Ask students to try moving that clause to the end of the sentence and also to the middle. How would they punctuate each sentence then? ("The scientist refused to believe that anything was wrong with her new formula for hand lotion, even after she grew three more fingers and a third arm," or "The scientist refused, even after she grew three more fingers and a third arm, to believe that anything was wrong with her new formula for hand lotion.")

Jake sat at his desk daydreaming and wondering, if squash could play squash, would they get squashed.

Jake sat at his desk daydreaming and wondering, "If squash could play squash, would they get squashed?"

Jake's thoughts should be treated as a quotation. He is speaking to himself, even if it is only in his thoughts. Therefore, quotations marks go around "If squash could play squash, would they get squashed?" Also, "If" is capitalized because it is the first word in the sentence being quoted.

Because the quotation is a question, it ends in a question mark. The question mark goes *before* the quotation marks, since the quotation itself is a question. If the sentence were a question, but the quotation itself were not, then the question mark would go outside the quotation marks. (Example: Do you like it when the teacher says, "Stop talking and get busy"?)

A Sentence a Day

Quotation marks, capitalization
question marks

Concerned about the fate of birds while the dragon was still lose. The Queen had all the birds in the Kingdom except magpies locked up in cages, she didn't like magpies.

Concerned about the fate of birds while the dragon was still loose, the queen had all the birds in the kingdom except magpies locked up in cages. She didn't like magpies.

The first part of the item is a sentence fragment. Change the period to a comma to fix the issue.

The second is a comma splice, or a type of run-on sentence. Two complete sentences cannot be separated by a comma. Use a semicolon, a period, or a conjunction. Some conjunctions don't necessarily require a comma ("because," "if," "though," "since"). Others do require a comma, such as coordinating conjunctions ("for," "and," "nor," "but," "or," "yet," "so," or FANBOYS).

"Lose" should be "loose." "Loose" rhymes with "caboose."

"The queen" and "kingdom" should not be capitalized since they are not specifically named.

This item is a good one for experimentation. Have students rewrite the sentence as many ways as possible, keeping the same meaning and recognizing that some versions will be better than others. (Example: Except for the magpies, which she didn't like, the queen was concerned about the fate of birds while the dragon was still loose. That is why she had all the birds in the kingdom locked up in cages.)

Renatta Reynaldo rested on the bed for a moment. Wishing she could change out of her beaded evening gown into jeans and a sweatshirt and go for a spin on her Harley Davidson Motorcycle.

Renatta Reynaldo rested on the bed for a moment, wishing she could change out of her beaded evening gown into jeans and a sweatshirt and go for a spin on her Harley Davidson motorcycle.

The item is really one sentence, not two. "Wishing she could change . . . and go for a spin on her Harley Davidson motorcycle" is really a dependent clause that should be part of the previous sentence.

"Harley Davidson" is capitalized because it is the brand name of the motorcycle. "Motorcycle" should not be capitalized.

A Sentence a Day

Fragments, capitalization

drive safe.

Drive safely.

The first word of a sentence should be capitalized.

"Drive" is a verb. "Safely" is an adverb. A verb needs an adverb to describe it. Therefore, the correct sentence is, "Drive safely." (Admittedly, people who insist on "Drive safely" are probably fighting a losing battle. "Drive safe" has become so common that it doesn't sound wrong to most people.)

"Safe" would be the word needed if you wanted to describe the *driver*, as in, "He was a safe driver." Then "safe" would be an adjective.

Well in my opinion pizza from pizza palooza makes a hole lot better snack than celery sticks and low-fat Cottage Cheese.

Well, in my opinion, pizza from Pizza Palooza makes a whole lot better snack than celery sticks and low-fat cottage cheese.

Introductory words such as "yes," "no," "oh," and "well" are followed by a comma. The "well" doesn't really add anything to the sentence and could be eliminated. If it is included, it should have a comma after it.

"Pizza Palooza" is capitalized because it is the name of a restaurant. "Cottage cheese" should not be capitalized as it is not the name of a certain brand.

"In my opinion" is a parenthetical expression that should be set off with a comma.

A "hole" is something dug in the ground. "Whole" is the word needed here.

A Sentence a Day

Commas, capitalization, word choice

Leafs fall in the Fall and leaf behind a blanket of red and orange covering the city streets every november. Well, maybe not in Antarctica.

Leaves fall in the fall and leave behind a blanket of red and orange covering the city streets every November . . . well, maybe not in Antarctica.

Many people are surprised that the seasons of the year are not capitalized. Months are capitalized; seasons are not.

The plural of "leaf" is "leaves." "Leave" is also a verb, as in "leave behind."

"Well, maybe not in Antarctica" is a sentence fragment. Rewriting it as, "Well, maybe this doesn't happen in Antarctica" is correct but seems to lack a little something—humor, perhaps?—that is implied in the original. Another solution is the one chosen above, to add ellipses and leave the fragment with the first sentence as an afterthought.

Mr. Tahini asked "what was wrong with me?" when I came into class wearing only a giant garbage bag with a bike chain belt around the middle and kleenex boxes as shoes.

Mr. Tahini asked what was wrong with me when I came into class wearing only a giant garbage bag with a bike chain belt around the middle and Kleenex boxes as shoes.

Because Mr. Tahini's exact words are not used, quotation marks are not needed. Neither is a question mark. (He didn't say, "What was wrong with me?") The sentence could include a direct quotation if it were altered to read like this:

Mr. Tahini asked, "What is wrong with you?" when I came into class wearing only a giant garbage bag with a bike chain belt around the middle and Kleenex boxes as shoes.

"Kleenex" is a brand name for tissues. Therefore, it should be capitalized.

A Sentence a Day

*Quotation marks,
capitalization*

My favorite thing at the circus is: the clowns, the magicians, the daring young men and women on the flying trapeze and the deep-fried Twinkies.

My favorite things at the circus are the clowns, the magicians, the daring young men and women on the flying trapeze, and the deep-fried Twinkies.

The speaker is not listing one favorite thing. He or she is listing favorite *things*. The verb should also be changed to "are" to agree with "things."

A colon is not used with a list when the list immediately follows a verb. To use a colon, the part of the sentence before the colon should really be a sentence itself. Here is an example:

Here is a list of my favorite things at the circus: the clowns, the magicians, the daring young men and women on the flying trapeze, and the deep-fried Twinkies.

Although the last comma in a series is usually considered optional, this sentence is clearer *with* it.

I don't know why everyone got so upset when I brought Harry my pet Tarantula to French Class and let him out of his cage to stretch his legs.

I don't know why everyone got so upset when I brought Harry, my pet tarantula, to French class and let him out of his cage to stretch his legs.

"Everyone" is one word, not two.

"My pet tarantula" is an appositive that interrupts the sentence to give more information about Harry. Therefore, it should be set off with commas.

"Harry" is capitalized because it is the tarantula's name, but "tarantula" should not be.

"French" is capitalized because it is made from the word "France." There is no reason to capitalize "class."

A Sentence a Day

Spelling, commas, capitalization

After Mrs. Fendlehessy gave detailed instructions for constructing a time machine Cecilia asked her to repeat them again.

After Mrs. Fendlehessy gave detailed instructions for constructing a time machine, Cecilia asked her to repeat them.

"After Mrs. Fendlehessy gave detailed instructions for constructing a time machine" is an introductory element (a clause). It should be followed by a comma.

There is no need to say "again." "Repeat" already means "say again." See if students can think of other examples of unnecessary words. (A few examples: "two twins," "7:00 p.m. in the evening," "advance planning.")

Drive East past the world's largest ball of twine then take a left at highway 41 and go North until you reach The Farm where my Cousin lives with his pet Emu and 63 Turtles.

Drive east past the world's largest ball of twine, and then take a left at Highway 41 and go north until you reach the farm where my cousin lives with his pet emu and 63 turtles.

Directions of the compass (east, north) should not be capitalized.

To fix the run-on sentence, add a comma and a coordinating conjunction between "twine" and "then."

There is no need to capitalize "the farm," "cousin," "emu," or "turtles." None of them are names of specific farms, cousins, emus, or turtles.

Street and road names like "Highway 41" should be capitalized.

A Sentence a Day

Capitalization, run-ons

No I don't like to eat at granola universe on green street, all it has on the menu is stuff like arugula and mushroom tarts and cabbage pudding.

No, I don't like to eat at Granola Universe on Green Street because all it has on the menu is food like arugula and mushroom tarts and cabbage pudding.

Introductory words such as "yes," "no," "oh," and "well" should be followed by a comma.

Names of restaurants and specific streets should be capitalized.

Two sentences separated by only a comma form a comma splice, a type of run-on sentence. A period or a semicolon could be used after "Green Street," or eliminating the comma and adding "because" also solves the problem.

Finally, the sentence could be improved by getting rid of the vague word "stuff."

Amiras prefered Summer vacation spot is Osage beach in Ozarks state park near Kansas city, MO but thats because of the cute life guard named Jonah that works there every year.

Amira's preferred summer vacation spot is Osage Beach in Ozarks State Park near Kansas City, Missouri, but that's because of the cute lifeguard named Jonah who works there every year.

Because it is a possessive, "Amira's" should end in an apostrophe and an *s*.

"Preferred" is the correct spelling.

Seasons of the year are not capitalized. Names of specific places are.

Generally, postal abbreviations of states should be confined to envelopes and lists. It's usually best to spell out the state when writing sentences.

In the corrected item, note that a comma should be placed after "Kansas City" and after "Missouri." (Most people remember the comma between the city and state. A comma should also be used after the state, abbreviated or not.)

"That's" is the correct spelling of the contraction for "that is."

"Lifeguard" is one word.

A person is a "who," not a "that."

A Sentence a Day

Apostrophes, capitalization, abbreviations, commas, spelling, word choice

Because there mother insisted they dress a like in pink dresses the twin girls always carried spare outfits in there jim bags and hurried into the restroom every morning to change.

Because their mother insisted they dress alike in pink dresses, the twin girls always carried spare outfits in their gym bags and hurried into the restroom every morning to change.

"Because their mother insisted they dress alike in pink dresses" is an introductory element (a clause) that should be set off with a comma.

"Their" is the word used whenever something or someone "belongs" to someone else. It is "*their* mother." It is "*their*" gym bag.

"Alike" is one word.

"Gym" is the correct spelling for the kind of bags the girls carried.

"I know you don't beleive there's actualy a job position called "odor judge" said Thor "but there is, and I'am gonna apply for it first thing tommorow."

"I know you don't believe there's actually a job position called 'odor judge,'" said Thor, "but there is, and I'm going to apply for it first thing tomorrow."

"Believe" follows the "*i* before *e* except after *c*" rule.

"Actually" has two *l*'s. "Tomorrow" has two *r*'s but only one *m*.

"I am" does not need an apostrophe. "I'm" does. There is no such word as "I'am."

"Gonna" should be "going to."

The sentence is interrupted with "said Thor" in the middle, so "said Thor" should be set off with commas on each side.

The phrase "odor judge" should have single quotation marks around it since it occurs within a quotation with double quotation marks.

A Sentence a Day

Spelling, apostrophes, commas, quotation marks

I'm not commited to the commitee, because it requires to much committment.

I'm not committed to the committee because it requires too much commitment.

This item has some tricky spelling issues. "Committed" and "committee" each have double *t*'s. "Commitment," however, does not.

A common error is to place a comma before "because" when it occurs in the middle of a sentence (in this case, introducing a subordinate clause). No comma is needed.

"Too" is the word needed to express an amount or degree, as in "too much commitment."

7th grade History teacher Mr. Carlander has a nite job as the drummer for the popular rock band, the hairy hecklers.

Seventh grade history teacher Mr. Carlander has a night job as the drummer for the popular rock band, the Hairy Hecklers.

When numbers occur as the first word in a sentence, they are spelled out.

School subjects are not capitalized, except for foreign languages. (Foreign languages are capitalized because they are formed from the names of countries.) Specific course titles such as "Introduction to Human Physiology 326" *are* capitalized.

"Night" is the correct spelling.

The band's name should be capitalized. (Students may argue that the real name of the band is "The Hairy Hecklers." That's a reasonable argument, though some stylebooks, such as the *Chicago Manual of Style*, advise *not* to capitalize articles before the name of a group, as in "the Beatles," not "The Beatles."

A Sentence a Day

Spelling, capitalization

Travel West on this road, it will eventually take you wear you want to go if wear you want to go is Podunk City.

Travel west on this road. It will eventually take you where you want to go, if where you want to go is Podunk City.

Directions are not capitalized. (If the sentence read, "I am going to travel to the West," it would be capitalized. Then "West" would refer to an area of the country, not a direction.)

The item is a comma splice, a type of run-on sentence. A comma cannot be used alone to separate two sentences. A period or a semicolon should be added after "road." An even better option would be to eliminate choppiness by rewriting the sentence altogether, perhaps like this: If you travel west on this road, it will eventually take you where you want to go, if where you want to go is Podunk City.

The word is "where," not "wear." "Wear" is what you do with clothing.

The comma before "if" is not absolutely necessary, but it does make the sentence a bit clearer.

Capitalization, run-ons,
word choice, commas

A Sentence a Day

Who seen the building plans for that new building the one they named the spa and salon center for pampered cats.

Who has seen the building plans for that new building, the one they named the Spa and Salon Center for Pampered Cats?

"Seen" always needs a helping verb before it—who *has* seen, who *will have* seen, who *was* seen, who *will be* seen, etc.

The sentence is a question, so it should end in a question mark.

The name of the new center should be capitalized.

"The one they named the Spa and Salon Center for Pampered Cats" is an appositive that gives more information about the building. Therefore, it should be preceded by a comma.

Jeanette decided to find out for herself why Miss Clutterbuck never let jaws her pit bull out of the backyard. It was not a good decision.

Jeanette decided to find out for herself why Miss Clutterbuck never let Jaws, her pit bull, out of the backyard. It was not a good decision.

"Herself" is one word, not two.

"Her pit bull" is an appositive that interrupts the sentence to give more information about "Jaws." Therefore, it should be set off with commas.

"Jaws" is the name of a specific pit bull. It should be capitalized.

Its not bad having a chef for a mom, except when she tries out recipes like the ones for: fudge-dipped mustard cookies or tangy vinegar milk shakes.

It's not bad having a chef for a mom, except when she tries out recipes like the ones for fudge-dipped mustard cookies or tangy vinegar milk shakes.

"It's" is the word needed when "It is" can be substituted in the sentence.

A colon is not necessary. It *would* be if the sentence read differently. "It's not bad having a chef for a mom, except when she tries out recipes like these: fudge-dipped mustard cookies or tangy vinegar milk shakes" is an example.

A Sentence a Day

Word choice, colons

To punish his younger brother for telling on him and getting him in trouble on the Bus, Edward smeared Chunky Peanut Butter under his brother's pillow dropped Happy Fish Tuna Surprise on the sheets and let in the Cat.

To punish his younger brother for telling on him and getting him in trouble on the bus, Edward smeared chunky peanut butter under his brother's pillow, dropped Happy Fish Tuna Surprise on the sheets(,) and let in the cat.

Items in a series should be separated by commas. The comma before the "and" is optional.

There is a lot of unnecessary capitalization going on in the item. There is no need to capitalize "bus" or "chunky peanut butter." "Happy Fish Tuna Surprise" is the brand name of a specific product, so it is capitalized. There is no need to capitalize "cat."

Jared use to be a good student and a great soccer player, however now he is only a great soccer player.

Jared used to be a good student and a great soccer player. However, now he is only a great soccer player.

Students frequently substitute "use to" for "used to," probably because it sounds like "use to" when they say it. It is properly spelled "used to."

The item is a comma splice. A comma cannot separate two sentences. A period or a semicolon is needed between "player" and "however."

Introductory words such as "however," "nevertheless," or "therefore" should be followed by a comma.

A Sentence a Day

Spelling, run-ons, commas

Kareem panicked when his pet hermit crab got lose and wandered out into the street, nearly missing the path of a Ford Truck.

Kareem panicked when his pet hermit crab got loose and wandered out into the street, nearly missing the path of a Ford truck.

"Lose" and "loose" are often confused. "Loose" both rhymes with and looks similar to "goose."

"Ford" is capitalized because it is a brand name. "Truck" is not part of the name. If the hermit crab had encountered a Ford Taurus, "Taurus" would have been capitalized because it *is* part of the brand name of a particular automobile.

"I don't know Astrid where you think your going in that outfit," remarked her mother, "but it certainly isn't out of this house."

"I don't know, Astrid, where you think you're going in that outfit," remarked her mother, "but it certainly isn't out of this house."

When a person is addressed, by name, the name is set off with commas.

"You're" should be used instead of "your" because "you're" is short for "you are."

I like pizza hamburgers tostadas and ice cream a hole lot better than the Organic garbanzo beans tofu lettuce and figs that my Mom always brings home, my brother still talks about and not in a good way the broccoli butterscotch chip cookies she made once.

I like pizza, hamburgers, tostadas, and ice cream a whole lot better than the organic garbanzo beans, tofu, lettuce, and figs that my mom always brings home. My brother still talks about—and not in a good way—the broccoli butterscotch chip cookies she made once.

This item has a number of problems. First, "whole" is the word needed, not "hole." A "hole" is something in the ground or in a doughnut.

Words in a series should be separated by commas. However, the final comma (the Oxford comma or the serial comma) is really optional, unless its elimination creates confusion in meaning.

There is no reason to capitalize "organic" or "mom."

The item is a run-on sentence. One option is to add a period after "home" and begin a new sentence with "My brother still talks about . . ."

"And not in a good way" is a parenthetical aside that interrupts the sentence. Dashes are appropriate to set it off. Parentheses are also acceptable.

The depressed dentist decided to stop flossing and treat himself to peanut brittle taffy licorish and caramel apples.

The depressed dentist decided to stop flossing and treat himself to peanut brittle, taffy, licorice(,) and caramel apples.

Commas are needed to separate items in a series.

"Licorice" is the correct spelling.

A Sentence a Day

Commas,
spelling

The dog and the cat was both sleeping on my backpack, so I couldn't possibly do my homework, that's why I never done it.

The dog and the cat were both sleeping on my backpack, so I couldn't possibly do my homework. That's why I never did it.

The first sentence has a plural subject ("dog and cat"), so it needs a plural verb—"were."

A period, a semicolon, or a conjunction is needed between "homework" and "that's" to fix the comma splice, which is a type of run-on sentence.

"Done" needs a helping verb with it, as in "I *have* not done my homework." With no helping verb, "did" is the word to use.

Allison should of asked before she borrowed you're diamond unicorn earrings because I know you're gonna be upset. Especially when you find out she lost them.

Allison should have asked before she borrowed your diamond unicorn earrings because I know you're going to be upset, especially when you find out she lost them.

Although the phrase *sounds* like "should of," it's really spelled "should have."

"You're" is a contraction of "you are." It should only be used when you can substitute "you are" in the sentence and have it make sense—as in "I know *you are* going to be upset." "Your" is used to show possession, as in "*your* diamond unicorn earrings."

"Gonna" should be spelled "going to."

"Especially when you find out she lost them" is a fragment that belongs with the previous sentence.

A Sentence a Day

Spelling, word choice, fragments

When he got a big pimple on his nose on the opening night of the play that stared him as a handsome hunk that was suppose to have all the girls falling in love with him.

When he got a big pimple on his nose on the opening night of the play that starred him as a handsome hunk who was supposed to have all the girls falling in love with him, Mario decided he didn't want to show up.

Although it is very long, the item above is still a sentence fragment. It needs to be finished. What *happened* right after Mario got the big pimple on his nose?

Girls may have "stared" at Mario, but he "starred" in the play.

People are referred to as "who," not "that."

It may sound like "suppose to," but the phrase is correctly spelled "supposed to."

Fragments, word choice,
spelling

A Sentence a Day

Sipping Cokes and strolling along, a truck suddenly appeared ahead of us.

Sipping Cokes and strolling along, we saw a truck suddenly appear ahead of us.

"Sipping Cokes and strolling along" is a dangling modifier. It sounds as though the truck is sipping Cokes and strolling along. That's because an introductory phrase should apply to the first noun after it—in this case, "truck." The sentence needs to be rewritten.

A Sentence a Day

Dangling modifiers

For all intensive purposes, Howard was really the teacher in the class, he new alot more then the real teacher.

For all intents and purposes, Howard was really the teacher in the class. He knew a lot more than the real teacher.

Many people mistakenly believe that the phrase is "for all intensive purposes." The phrase is really "for all intents and purposes."

The item is a comma splice, a type of run-on sentence. A period, a semicolon, or a conjunction is needed after "class." Some conjunctions don't necessarily require a comma ("because," "if," "though," "since"). Others do require a comma, such as coordinating conjunctions ("for," "and," "nor," "but," "or," "yet," "so," or FANBOYS).

"Knew" is the word needed, not "new."

"A lot" is two words, not one.

"Than" is the correct word in this sentence because it refers to a comparison between Howard and the teacher. "Then" refers to time/order or means "in that case," "as a necessary consequence," "besides," and some other similar things. "Upon arrival, I knew I had a better costume than anyone else at the party, and then I won the costume contest."

"I'm running away to join the circus and become a clown," said Amelia. I realy hope the other clowns will except me, share there big rubber lips, give me tips on makeup, ect."

"I'm running away to join the circus and become a clown," said Amelia. "I really hope the other clowns will accept me, share their big rubber lips, give me tips on makeup, etc."

"Really" has two *l*'s.

"Except" means "all but this." "Accept" is the word needed here.

It should be "*their* big rubber lips." "Their" is used to show possession.

"Etc." is really pronounced "*et* cetera," not "*eck* cetera." It is spelled that way, too, with the *t* coming before the *c*.

Quotation marks are needed before "I," as quotation marks come in pairs.

A Sentence a Day

Spelling, word choice, quotation marks

Jake's mother collects antiques and is looking for a mahogany desk suitable for a woman with thick legs and large drawers.

Jake's mother collects antiques and is looking for a mahogany desk with thick legs and large drawers, suitable for a woman.

The problem with this item is the placement of "with thick legs and large drawers."

By placing the phrase after "woman," it sounds as though she is looking for a woman with thick legs and large drawers.

Dangling
modifiers

A Sentence a Day

Zachary ate a apple and a orange and then decided hed had enuff healthy food, he called perfect pizza palace and ordered a anchovy and pepperoni pizza with extra cheeze.

Zachary ate an apple and an orange and then decided he'd had enough healthy food. He called Perfect Pizza Palace and ordered an anchovy and pepperoni pizza with extra cheese.

"An" is used with words that begin with a vowel sound, such as "apple," "orange," and "anchovy."

"He'd" needs an apostrophe, since it is a contraction of "he had."

"Enough" doesn't have any *f*'s in it.

"Perfect Pizza Palace" is the name of a specific pizzeria, so it should be capitalized.

"Cheese" may sound like it has a *z* in it, but it doesn't.

The item is a comma splice, a type of run-on sentence. A comma can't be used to separate complete sentences. Use a period, a semicolon, or a conjunction. Some conjunctions don't necessarily require a comma ("because," "if," "though," "since"). Others do require a comma, such as coordinating conjunctions ("for," "and," "nor," "but," "or," "yet," "so," or FANBOYS).

A Sentence a Day

Word choice, apostrophes, spelling capitalization, run-ons

Calvin put down his money and signs up for the "Teenagers Who Don't Get an Allowance" bowling turnament.

Calvin put down his money and signed up for the "Teenagers Who Don't Get an Allowance" bowling tournament.

The item above switches tenses. It starts out with a verb in past tense ("put") and switches to present tense ("signs"). The sentence should be rewritten so that all the verbs are in past tense.

"Tournament" is the correct spelling.

It is not incorrect to remove the quotes around "Teenagers Who Don't Get an Allowance." It's the name of the tournament, but since it's a rather odd name, the quotation marks help distinguish it as a name. It is also possible that "bowling tournament" is part of the official name of the event. Therefore, "Teenagers Who Don't Get an Allowance Bowling Tournament" should also be considered correct.

The mischievious mannequins came to life when the department store closed, they changed out of their silk dresses into shorts and sweatshirts and playing baseball in the cosmetics department.

The mischievous mannequins came to life when the department store closed. They changed out of their silk dresses into shorts and sweatshirts and played baseball in the cosmetics department.

The item is a comma splice, a type of run-on sentence. A comma cannot be used to separate two sentences. Use a period, a semicolon, or a conjunction. Some conjunctions don't necessarily require a comma ("because," "if," "though," "since"). Others do require a comma, such as coordinating conjunctions ("for," "and," "nor," "but," "or," "yet," "so," or FANBOYS).

"Mischievous" is often misspelled (and mispronounced) with an extra *i* after the *v*.

Regarding verb form, the second sentence has a problem with parallelism. The verbs are "changed" and "playing." "Playing" should be changed to "played" to match the form of the first verb and to help the whole thing make sense. (Ask students to read the incorrect version aloud, and they will likely stumble on the second sentence. Whether they realize it or not, they intuitively know that something is wrong.)

A Sentence a Day

Run-ons, spelling, verb form

Don't let their cuteness fool you; these adorable fluffy puppys and kittys from Dr. Doominskis lab are extreemly deadly and can kill you with just one bite.

Don't let their cuteness fool you; these adorable, fluffy puppies and kitties from Dr. Doominski's lab are extremely deadly and can kill you with just one bite.

Students may see a semicolon and assume it is wrong. It is not. A semicolon can be used to separate two closely related sentences. (Some believe that the semicolon is slowly disappearing. Some newspapers and magazines rarely, if ever, use it.)

"Puppies" and "kitties" follow a rule common in words ending in a consonant and a *y*: change the *y* to *i* and add "es."

"Extremely" is the correct spelling.

Dr. Doominski should be possessive, since the lab "belongs" to him. Therefore, an apostrophe should appear before the *s*.

My brother Leo, spent the hole morning trying to turn the shower stall into a time machine.

My brother Leo spent the whole morning trying to turn the shower stall into a time machine.

There is no need for a comma after "Leo." People often insert a comma between the subject and verb of a sentence. They should not.

"Leo" is a one-word appositive. Commas are usually eliminated around one-word appositives, but it would not be incorrect to place a comma both before *and* after "Leo."

A "hole" belongs in the ground. "Whole" refers to all of something.

"If you don't volunteer to clean up the mess you made during the food fight," said principle lazoria, "You will spend your next 5 lunch periods eating cold oatmeal in The Office."

"If you don't volunteer to clean up the mess you made during the food fight," said Principal Lazoria, "you will spend your next five lunch periods eating cold oatmeal in the office."

"Principal" is the word to use for a school administrator, not "principle." It is not capitalized except when used with the principal's name, as in "Principal Lazoria."

Principal Lazoria really speaks only one sentence. (Well, he probably speaks *a lot* more of them during this incident, but in the item above, he speaks only one.) It is interrupted with "said Principal Lazoria." Therefore, the second part of the quotation should not be capitalized.

Numbers smaller than ten should be spelled out, not written as numerals.

There is no need to capitalize "the office," unless perhaps you're speaking of the television show by the same name.

On the campain trail, the excentric politician wore a santa suit and handed out green beens, little packets of catsup, and money tied with brightly, colored ribon.

On the campaign trail, the eccentric politician wore a Santa suit and handed out green beans, little packets of catsup(,) and money tied with brightly colored ribbon.

When it comes to spelling, "campaign" is a doozy of a word. It's a wonder anyone ever gets it right. "Eccentric" isn't easy, either, since it really sounds like it *should* have an x. "Beans" and "ribbon" are much easier.

"Santa" should be capitalized because it's a name.

There is no reason to put a comma between "brightly" and "colored." (One test: try putting "and" between the words—"brightly" *and* "colored ribbon." If "and" doesn't sound right, a comma isn't needed.)

A Sentence a Day

Spelling, capitalization, commas

Mr. Pennybroke turned to his son and asked "Remember that new video game you want me to buy for you, the one that is so charmingly titled Do You Want to Harass Your Parents."

Mr. Pennybroke turned to his son and asked, "Remember that new video game you want me to buy for you, the one that is so charmingly titled 'Do You Want to Harass Your Parents?'?"

Correcting this one takes some real care with details. First, a comma must separate Mr. Pennybroke's actual words from the introductory part of the sentence. Therefore, a comma should follow "said."

"Do You Want to Harass Your Parents?" should have quotation marks around it because it is a title. However, because it occurs in a quotation that already *has* quotation marks, the quotation marks should be single.

The video's title itself is a question, so a question mark should be placed inside the single quotes, but the whole sentence Mr. Pennybroke speaks is also a question. That means a question mark also goes at the end of the sentence. (Yes, it looks very strange. If students get this right, they surely deserve a pat on the back.)

Miss Glenflinkenhaven does two strange things, she insisted on wearing a giant hat made of fruit when she goes grocery shopping, and she plays the harp with her tows.

Miss Glenflinkenhaven does two strange things: she insists on wearing a giant hat made of fruit when she goes grocery shopping, and she plays the harp with her toes.

"Miss Glenflinkenhaven does two strange things" should be followed by a colon. The colon means "Note what follows." (A dash would also be acceptable.)

The entire sentence moves back and forth between present and past tense. It starts out in present tense, so it should continue in present tense.

"Toes" are those appendages on our feet—and also on Miss Glenflinkenhaven's.

A Sentence a Day

Colons, verb tense,
word choice

Never hug a hibble, in a hibble habble horper, never kiss a kibble, in a kibble kabble korper.

Never hug a hibble in a hibble habble horper, and never kiss a kibble in a kibble kabble korper.

Okay, the sentence makes no sense unless you know what a hibble habble horper or a kibble kabble korper is. Even with such nonsensical words, we can tell that the item is a run-on sentence and needs a period, semicolon, or coordinating conjunction between "horper" and "never." It is easy to tell that the item is really two sentences, even if no one has ever even *thought* of hugging a hibble.

There is no need for the commas after "hibble" and "kibble."

Irregardless of your opinion, you have to go to aunt ethels doily crocheting party next Week on Tuesday.

Regardless of your opinion, you have to go to Aunt Ethel's doily crocheting party next week on Tuesday.

"Irregardless" may be in the dictionary, along with "ain't," but it is noted as "nonstandard." "Regardless" is the word to use.

Aunt Ethel should be capitalized because it is being used as her name.

An apostrophe should be placed before the *s* in "Aunt Ethel's" to show possession. The doily crocheting party "belongs" to Aunt Ethel.

The word "week" is not capitalized, but names of days of the week are.

A Sentence a Day

Word choice, capitalization, apostrophes

Hey, man!
The college you are president of sounds like really cool and stuff, and you know like I totally want to get into it and like find a career that's all about like success and stuff.

Dear President Malloy:
I would like to apply to your college to pursue a career in astrophysics.

Use a formal salutation such as "Dear," not "hey" or "hi."

A colon follows the salutation in a business or formal letter.

It is not a good idea to assume the president is a man. Taking time to find out the president's name is much smarter.

Slang has its place. We all use it. However, we should all know when it's appropriate and when it is not. A college application is not the place for it. The sentence needs to be rewritten.

"Like" and "you know" are filler words in this sentence and should be deleted.

A Sentence a Day

My Grandpa, he worries alot about bed bugs and nuclear war.

My grandpa worries a lot about bed bugs and nuclear war.

"Grandpa" is only capitalized if it's being used as a name: "We love Grandpa."

"My grandpa, he" is a double subject. There is no need to say "he."

"A lot" is two words.

A Sentence a Day

Double subjects,
spelling

Blake wanted ice cream. And so the babysitter gave him some. And then she tried to get him to eat carrots, but he wouldn't. And so she poured some chocalate syrup on them. And then he did.

Blake wanted ice cream, so the babysitter gave him some. Then she tried to get him to eat carrots, but he wouldn't, so she poured some chocolate syrup on them. Then he did.

There are other ways to "fix" the item above. The problem is the choppiness of all those sentences starting with "and so" and "and then."

"Chocolate" is the correct spelling.

Blake's babysitter is obviously a seasoned professional.

Patrice lead the lead pencil boycott because he was a good leeder

Patrice led the lead pencil boycott because he was a good leader.

"Lead" and "led" are often confused, and it's no wonder. "Lead," pronounced to rhyme with "head," is a kind of metal. Another word that *sounds* the same is "led," which is the past tense of the verb "lead" (pronounced "leed"), as in, "You can lead a horse to water, but you can't make him drink."

A simpler way to think of it: the spelling "led" is used for only one thing—the past tense of the verb "lead," as in, "He led them into battle."

The sentence should end in a period.

A Sentence a Day

125

Word choice,
spelling, periods

Pickles my "orange tabby cat" clawed her way through the new screen door to chase a couple a robins who weren't at all eager to be somebodys dinner.

Pickles, my orange tabby cat, clawed her way through the new screen door to chase a couple of robins who weren't at all eager to be somebody's dinner.

There is a sad trend in quotation marks. They are appearing everywhere, for no good reason. Restaurants advertise spinach salad with "feta" cheese. Clothing stores advertise new shipments of "turtlenecks." Such quotation marks are completely unnecessary, as are the quotation marks around "orange tabby cat."

"My orange tabby cat" is an appositive that interrupts the sentence to give more information about Pickles. It should be set off with commas.

The phrase "couple of" may sound like "couple a" when we say it, but that's not the way it is spelled.

"Somebody" needs an apostrophe after it to show possession. It's a dinner that "belongs" to somebody.

Harrison looked at his father and goes, "Yuk! Dad why do you always have to ware those plaid golf pants when my friends are around."

Harrison looked at his father and said, "Yuk! Dad, why do you always have to wear those plaid golf pants when my friends are around?"

People "say," not "go." Harrison looked at his father and "said."

Harrison is directly addressing Dad, so "Dad" needs a comma after it.

Harrison is also asking Dad a question. Therefore, a question mark goes after his question, inside the quotation marks.

"Wear" is the correct spelling.

A Sentence a Day

Word choice, commas, question marks, spelling

No it's not O.K. with us if your little sister & her friends want to go thru our haunted house with a flashlite because there afraid of the dark.

No, it's not okay with us if your little sister and her friends want to go through our haunted house with a flashlight because they're afraid of the dark.

Introductory words such as "yes," "no," "well," and "oh" are followed by a comma.

In all except the most informal writing, "okay" and "and" should be spelled out.

Although "thru" and "lite" are starting to appear everywhere, the correct spellings are "through" and "light." "Flashlight" follows the same principle.

"They're" is the correct spelling of the contraction for "they are."

Ingrid did'nt do good on the rocket science test, and she reminded her self to study next time.

Ingrid didn't do well on the rocket science test, and she reminded herself to study next time.

"Didn't" is a contraction for "did not." The apostrophe replaces "o" in "not," so it goes between "n" and "t."

To describe how someone *did* something, "well" is the word to use, not "good."

"Herself" is one word.

The Complex Question or **Loaded Question**

"There isn't nothing you can do to fix that busted lamp," said Jenna to her little brother. "You might as well leave home now.

"There isn't anything you can do to fix that broken lamp," said Jenna to her little brother. "You might as well leave home now."

Double negatives are not a good thing. Jenna should be saying, "There isn't anything you can do . . ."

"Busted" is considered slang. "Broken" is preferred.

Quotation marks are needed after "now." Quotation marks come in pairs.

If students argue that a direct quotation should quote people accurately, even if they are using double negatives and slang, they are correct. If we assume that Jenna is being quoted accurately, nothing is wrong with the item, except for the missing quotation marks at the end.

Well him and me gotta go to get some new battries for are auto-matic pencil washer before we can do are homewrok.

Well, he and I have to go get some new batteries for our auto-matic pencil washer before we can do our homework.

A comma should be placed after introductory words such as "yes," "oh," "no," and "well." "Well" is often stuck in as a filler and serves no purpose. The sentence would be even more improved if "well" were eliminated altogether.

"Him and me gotta go" should be replaced with "he and I have to go." (A test: rephrase the sentence so that the subject is singular, and see which pronoun sounds right. "Him has to go"? "Me has to go"? No.)

"Batteries" and "homework" are the correct spellings.

"Our" is the word needed, not "are"—even though the spoken "our" often sounds like "are." "Our" is used to show possession.

A Sentence a Day

Commas, unnecessary words, pronouns, spelling, word choice while the class takes a test, Mrs. Melktoste is reading an article called how to deal with impossible studnets. It is in the magazine teaching today.

While the class takes a test, Mrs. Melktoste is reading an article called "How to Deal with Impossible Students." It is in the magazine *Teaching Today*.

The sentence should begin with a capital letter.

Titles of magazine articles should be placed in quotation marks. The first, last, and all important words should be capitalized.

"Students" is the correct spelling.

The names of magazines and books are capitalized and placed in italics. (When handwritten, they should be underlined.) However, because publications differ in their policies, you should review their style guides for specific usage rules.

The bigest taco in the entire universe.

Penelope was so hungry she thought she could eat the biggest taco in the entire universe.

The item above is a sentence fragment and can be corrected in many ways. The important thing is that the item needs a verb.

"Biggest" is the correct spelling.

A Sentence a Day

Fragments,
spelling

"did you remember to write your research paper" asked Mr. thorn-whimple. "oops" said brian.

"Did you remember to write your research paper?" asked Mr. Thornwhimple.
 "Oops," said Brian.

In dialogue, a new paragraph begins with each change of speakers.

Mr. Thornwhimple asks a question, so his words should end with a question mark.

Both quotations should begin with capital letters.

"Mr. Thornwhimple" and "Brian" are proper nouns that should be capitalized.

"Oops" should be separated from the dialogue tag "said Brian" with a comma. (An exclamation point would also be appropriate.)

Witch one is more slower: a turtel with a limp or a groggy snail?

Which one is slower: a turtle with a limp or a groggy snail?

A "witch" rides a broom. "Which" is the word needed here.

The three forms of "slow" are "slow" (to describe one thing), "slower" (to compare two things), and "slowest" (to compare three things.) "More" is unnecessary with "slower."

"Turtle" is the correct spelling.

A good follow-up is to have students try adding to the sentence so that "slowest" is the correct form of the word, as in "Which one is slowest: a turtle with a limp, a groggy snail, or the clock during last period of the school day?"

A Sentence a Day

Word choice,
unnecessary words spelling

The family cancelled the trip to the beach due to the fact that fish was raining from the sky.

The family cancelled the trip to the beach because fish were raining from the sky.

An alternate spelling of "cancelled" is "canceled."

A singular noun pairs with "was." A plural noun pairs with "were." Because "fish" is plural, the verb to use with it is "were."

"Due to the fact that" is not really wrong, but it is a cumbersome phrase. "Because" works much better.

Verb form,
unnecessary words

A Sentence a Day

The new teachers plan was based on her beleif that kids' really love to do grammer exercises in english class.

The new teacher's plan was based on her belief that kids really love to do grammar exercises in English class.

The plan "belongs" to the teacher. Therefore, "teacher's" needs an apostrophe before the *s*. (If the plan belonged to a lot of teachers, the apostrophe would go after the *s*.)

"Belief" follows the "*i* before *e* except after *c*" rule.

"Kids" is not a possessive and should not have an apostrophe.

"English" should be capitalized because it is the name of a language.

"Grammar" ends in "ar," not "er."

A Sentence a Day

Apostrophes, spelling, capitalization

When the band started playing a polka at the barnyard wedding all the foul in attendence did the chicken dance.

When the band started playing a polka at the barnyard wedding, all the fowl in attendance did the chicken dance.

"When the band started playing a polka at the barnyard wedding" is an introductory element (a clause) that should be followed by a comma.

"Foul" describes a smell. "Fowl" is used to refer to chickens. (The fowl could smell foul, of course.)

There is a "dance" in the word "attendance."

Mrs. Elmwood wondered why the dog was green and hairless after it came out of her sons bedroom, but she new that it wasn't her darling little charlies fault cuz he never told a lie or did anything rong.

Mrs. Elmwood wondered why the dog was green and hairless after it came out of her son's bedroom, but she knew that it wasn't her darling little Charlie's fault because he never told a lie or did anything wrong.

There are two possessives in the sentence: *son's* bedroom and *Charlie's* fault.

"New" might describe the dog's look, but "knew" is the word needed after "she."

"Little," "because," and "wrong" are the correct spellings of the words needed in the last part of the sentence.

A Sentence a Day

Apostrophes, word choice, spelling

I couldn't hardly see the rode cuz it was raining cats and dogs.

I could hardly see the road because it was raining cats and dogs.

"Could hardly" is the correct phrase, not "couldn't hardly." ("Couldn't hardly" is considered a double negative.)

"Road" is the word needed here. "Rode" is the past tense of "ride."

"Because" is the correct spelling.

To improve the sentence even further, students might try to eliminate the cliché, "raining cats and dogs." See if they can come up with more original ways to describe how hard it was raining.

David was furious because he didn't no where his lobster costume was at.

David was furious because he didn't know where his lobster costume was.

"Know" is the word needed, not "no."

"At" is an unnecessary preposition at the end of the sentence.

A Sentence a Day

Word choice, unnecessary words

Because he didn't want to eat his desert in the desert.

Because he didn't want to eat his dessert in the desert, Aaron decided to put his butterscotch pudding in the cooler.

"Dessert" is a sweet something at the end of a meal. A "desert" is a hot and dry place.

The item is a sentence fragment. A good follow-up exercise is to have students correct the fragment in at least five different ways, with "because" in the middle of the sentence as well as at the beginning of the sentence.

Duffy literally jumped out of his skin when he heard the door to his room open at midnight.

Duffy jumped out of his skin when he heard the door to his room open at midnight.

If Duffy *literally* jumped out of his skin, he would be a skeleton. There is an odd trend to use "literally" in a way that makes no sense. "Literally" means "actually." Did Duffy *actually* jump out of his skin? Probably not.

"Jumped out of his skin" is a cliché. The sentence would be improved even further if rewritten to describe Duffy's fear in a fresh, new way. A good follow-up activity is to have students try describing his fear without using "jumped out of his skin."

A Sentence a Day

Word choice, clichés

I'm tired of setting hear, and I hope this boring class will soon be over with so I can excape," exclaimed Seneca!

"I'm tired of sitting here, and I hope this boring class will soon be over so I can escape!" exclaimed Seneca.

People "sit." They "set" things down on tables.

"Hear" is what our ears do. "Here" is where Seneca is sitting.

The word is "escape," not "excape."

Quotation marks come in pairs. They are needed at the beginning and end of a quotation.

There is no need for "with" after the word "over."

In a quotation, the exclamation point goes after the sentence that is an exclamation—and before the quotation marks.

Curled up in his underwear drawer, Abel saw that his new kitten had finally settled down.

Curled up in his underwear drawer, Abel's new kitten had finally settled down.

Dangling modifiers can be unintentionally funny. Abel, of course, is not curled up in his underwear drawer. The cat is. "Curled up in his underwear drawer" must refer to the next noun in the sentence, so that noun should be "kitten," not Abel. (In the incorrect version, "Abel" is a noun. In the correct version, "Abel's" is an adjective describing the noun "kitten.")

A Sentence a Day

Dangling
modifiers

The squirrel scampered into the house, jumped on the table, and landed on are Thanksgiving Turkey.

The squirrel scampered into the house, jumped on the table, and landed on our Thanksgiving turkey.

Students often mistake "are" for "our," probably because many pronounce the words almost identically.

"Thanksgiving" should be capitalized because it is the name of a holiday. "Turkey" should not be capitalized just because it follows "Thanksgiving."

Laughing loudly at Earl's joke, the green Jell-O flew into the air when Gavin tripped.

Laughing loudly at Earl's joke, Gavin tripped and sent green Jell-O flying into the air.

There are many ways to correct this sentence, which has Jell-O laughing loudly—an unlikely occurrence. "Laughing loudly at Earl's joke" is a dangling modifier. As written, it describes Jell-O. The sentence must be rewritten so that it describes "Gavin," the one who really did the laughing.

"Jell-O" is capitalized because it is a brand name. As a generic gelatin dessert, it is spelled jello.

A Sentence a Day

Dangling modifiers, capitalization

When the hostess told the boys they would have to put on shoes before they could be seated in the restraunt.

When the hostess told the boys they would have to put on shoes before they could be seated in the restaurant, they decided to walk down the street and grab hot dogs from the hot dog cart.

The item above is a fragment and needs to be completed. What happened when the hostess told the boys they would have to put on shoes? A good follow-up activity is to have the students try to complete the sentence at least three different ways.

"Restaurant" is the proper spelling for this difficult word.

The people at the costume party, they complimented one another on their hideously, ugly masks as they enjoyed ordervs made of bat wings and frog eyeballs.

The people at the costume party complimented one another on their hideously ugly masks as they enjoyed hors d'oeuvres made of bat wings and frog eyeballs.

"The people at the costume party" and "they" are the same thing. There is no need for a double subject here. "They" should be omitted.

A test to check if there should be a comma between "hideously" and "ugly" is to try saying "and" between the two words. If "and" works, a comma is needed. In this case, "hideously and ugly masks" does not sound right.

Does anyone really know how to spell "hors d'oeuvres"? Challenge your students to master this very, very difficult word.

Quinn wouldn't be quite when the teacher said he was waisting the hole Class period texting his freinds, about the Animatronic Gargoyle he had one in a online contest.

Quinn wouldn't be quiet when the teacher said he was wasting the whole class period texting his friends about the animatronic gargoyle he had won in an online contest.

The item above is a mess of incorrect word choices and spelling errors. After the students have corrected the sentence, challenge them to write a new sentence using "quite," "waist," "hole," and "one" correctly.

There is no need for a comma after "friends."

The words "class," "animatronic," and "gargoyle" are used as common nouns in the sentence and should not be capitalized.

"An" is used before words beginning with a vowel, as in "an online contest."

When her Dad asked her, "why she came home so late," Mindy studdered, "well my friends and I went to . . . uh . . . bible study . . . and . . . uh . . . I guess we lost track of time."

When her dad asked her why she came home so late, Mindy stuttered, "Well, my friends and I went to . . . uh . . . Bible study . . . and . . . uh . . . I guess we lost track of time."

In this case, "dad" should not be capitalized because "her" is used with it. In other words, "dad" is not being used as a noun of direct address.

The first part of the sentence is an indirect quotation and does not need quotation marks. "Why she came home so late" are *not* the words that came out of Mindy's dad's mouth.

"Stuttered" has double *t*'s, not double *d*'s.

Introductory words such as "yes," "no," "oh," and "well" should be followed by commas.

"Bible" is the name of a book and should be capitalized.

A Sentence a Day

Capitalization, quotation marks, spelling, commas

Please tell me that singing this peace of paper will cancel further deliverys of these garden gnomes, which I never ordered, I also never ordered the bags of elephant manure.

Please tell me that signing this piece of paper will cancel further deliveries of these garden gnomes, which I never ordered. I also never ordered the bags of elephant manure.

There is a big difference between "singing" and "signing," just as there is a big difference between "piece" and "peace."

The plural of many words that end in a consonant and *y* is formed by changing the *y* to *i* and adding "es."

The item is a comma splice, a type of run-on sentence. Two sentences cannot be separated by a comma alone. A period is needed after the first "ordered." Or use a semicolon or a conjunction. Some conjunctions don't necessarily require a comma ("because," "if," "though," "since"). Others do require a comma, such as coordinating conjunctions ("for," "and," "nor," "but," "or," "yet," "so," or FANBOYS).

Nekita didn't care that she wasn't chosen to go to hollywood after her audition for American Idol, she didn't want to go anyways.

Nekita didn't care that she wasn't chosen to go to Hollywood after her audition for *American Idol*. She didn't want to go anyway.

"Hollywood" is capitalized because it is the name of a certain city.

As the title of a television show, *American Idol* should be italicized or underlined. (Some sources recommend using quotation marks instead of italics for television show titles.)

The correct term is "anyway," not "anyways."

A Sentence a Day

Capitalization, italics, word choice

After thinking it over carefully Verna decided she did'nt want either rasberry sauce or choclate sirup on her macaroni and cheese.

After thinking it over carefully, Verna decided she didn't want either raspberry sauce or chocolate syrup on her macaroni and cheese.

"After thinking it over carefully" is an introductory element (a phrase). It should be followed by a comma.

The apostrophe in "didn't" goes between the *n* and the *t*.

"Raspberry," to the surprise of many, has a *p* in it.

"Chocolate" has two *o*'s.

"Syrup" has a *y*, not an *i*.

Because the sun was in my eyes I didn't see the pothole in the road so I hit it with my frunt tire and flipped over my handle bars and then landed with my face firmly planted on the asphalt, I felt really stupid besides that my face hurt.

Because the sun was in my eyes, I didn't see the pothole in the road. I hit it with my front tire and flipped over my handlebars, landing with my face firmly planted on the asphalt. I felt really stupid. Besides that, my face hurt.

There are a number of ways to fix this run-on sentence. Above is one example.

"Front" and "handlebars" are the correct spellings.

A Sentence a Day

Run-ons, spelling

I wish I had never went to the party, witch was a nightmair, alot of people whom were their got food poisoning from Hannas home made cucumber dip.

I wish I had never gone to the party, which was a nightmare. A lot of people who were there got food poisoning from Hanna's homemade cucumber dip.

"Went" should never be used with a helping verb. "Gone" is the word needed after "had."

"Which," "nightmare," "a lot," and "homemade" are the correct spellings needed.

The item is a comma splice, a type of run-on sentence. A period is needed between "nightmare" and "a lot." There are other possibilities, too, such as eliminating the comma after "nightmare" and adding "because."

The correct word needed here is "there," not "their."

The correct word needed here is "who," not "whom." Something to remember about using the pronouns "who" and "whom" is that "who" refers to the subject of a sentence, and "whom" refers to the object of a verb or a preposition. To determine which one to use, substitute "he," "she," or "they" for "who" or "whom." If it sounds correct, use "who." Then substitute "him," "her," or "them" for "who" or "whom." If it sounds correct, use "whom." In this example, substitute "they" for "whom": "They were there." That sounds correct. Then substitute "them" for "whom": "Them were there." That sounds incorrect, so you wouldn't use "whom."

"Hanna's" should have an apostrophe since it is a possessive. The dip "belongs" to her.

It looked like someone sent a bunch of banana's through a blender and then through the whole thing on top of the toyota.

It looked like someone sent a bunch of bananas through a blender and then threw the whole thing on top of the Toyota.

"Bananas" does not need an apostrophe. The bananas don't possess anything.

"Threw" is the spelling needed when something is tossed.

"Toyota" should be capitalized because it is a car's brand name.

A Sentence a Day

Apostrophes, word choice, capitalization

If you sit at you're computer two much. You might turn into a mouse potato.

If you sit at your computer too much, you might turn into a mouse potato.

"Your" is the word needed, not "you're."

"Too" is the word needed, not "two."

The first "sentence" is a fragment. It is really an introductory element (a clause) that should be part of the next sentence.

Are Science class with Mr Fentiman is so boaring, my Math class would be boaring, two, but are teacher is miss fazio and she is so beutaful that I don't mind math at all.

Our science class with Mr. Fentiman is so boring. My math class would be boring, too, but our teacher is Miss Fazio, and she is so beautiful that I don't mind math at all.

"Are" should be "our." "Boaring" should be "boring." "Beutaful" should be "beautiful."

"Two" should be "too" because it is used in the sense of "also."

"Mr." needs a period because it's an abbreviation for "mister."

"Science" and "math" should not be capitalized. The only school subjects capitalized are languages (English, French) or specific course names (Introduction to Algebra).

A Sentence a Day

Word choice, spelling, abbreviations, capitalization

My leg fell a sleep when I was sitting on the grass waiting for Mom to finish talking to my teacher as Hank Steel, the cutest guy in the world, motions for me to sit next to him on the bleachers, I try to stand up and fell flat on my face.

My leg fell asleep when I was sitting on the grass waiting for Mom to finish talking to my teacher as Hank Steel, the cutest guy in the world, motioned for me to sit next to him on the bleachers. I tried to stand up and fell flat on my face.

"Asleep" is one word, not two.

The item switches back and forth between past and present tense. Since it starts out in past tense ("leg *fell* asleep"), it should stay in past tense. "Motions" should be "motioned" and "try" should be "tried."

The sentence is also a comma splice, a type of run-on sentence. The comma after "bleachers" should be a period. Or use a semicolon or a conjunction. Some conjunctions don't necessarily require a comma ("because," "if," "though," "since"). Others do require a comma, such as coordinating conjunctions ("for," "and," "nor," "but," "or," "yet," "so," or FANBOYS).

When the toilet made a wierd gurgling sound while I dried my hands, I thought to myself, "please let me get out before it blows" when I left, I herd a enormus explosion.

When the toilet made a weird gurgling sound while I dried my hands, I thought to myself, "Please let me get out before it blows." When I left, I heard an enormous explosion.

"Please" should be capitalized since it is the first word of the sentence in the quotation.

The sentence is a run-on. A period is needed before "when."

"Herd" refers to cattle, not what a person does with ears. The correct spelling here is "heard."

"An" is used before words beginning with a vowel, as in "an enormous explosion."

"Enormous" and "weird" are the correct spellings.

A Sentence a Day

Capitalization, run-ons, word choice, spelling

I wonder if Rattle Snakes have any rythim?

I wonder if rattlesnakes have any rhythm.

"Rattlesnakes" is one word, not two.

"Rhythm" is the correct spelling. In this case, *y* is used as a vowel.

There is no need to capitalize the common noun "rattlesnakes."

The sentence is not a question. It is a statement. A question would be, "Do you ever wonder if rattlesnakes have any rhythm?" or "Do rattlesnakes have any rhythm?"

A Sentence a Day

My Dentist says that I'm going to loose my teeth if I don't start flossing I wonder if theres such a thing as choclate Dental floss.

My dentist says that I'm going to lose my teeth if I don't start flossing. I wonder if there's such a thing as chocolate dental floss.

"Dentist" should not be capitalized. There is no reason to capitalize "dental," either.

"Lose" is the correct spelling. (If she doesn't floss, however, she might get a *loose* tooth.)

The item is a run-on sentence. One option is to add a period after "flossing" and begin a new sentence with "I wonder if . . ."

"There's" should have an apostrophe before the *s*. It is a contraction of "there is."

There are two *o*'s in "chocolate."

A Sentence a Day

Capitalization, spelling, run-ons

If we have to eat Tuna casserole one more night for dinner. I'm going to screem.

If we have to eat tuna casserole one more night for dinner, I'm going to scream.

"Tuna" should not be capitalized.

"If we have to eat tuna casserole one more night for dinner" is a fragment. It should be part of the next sentence, separated by a comma.

"Scream" is the correct spelling for what someone does after eating tuna casserole for too many nights straight.

Benny our nieghbor that likes to get up at 5 evry saturday morning to mow the lawn and drive all the nieghbors crazy.

Benny, our neighbor who likes to get up at 5:00 every Saturday morning to mow the lawn and drive all the neighbors crazy, is not the most popular guy on our block.

The item above is a fragment. Everything that follows "Benny" is part of a long appositive giving more information about "Benny." After the appositive, the sentence needs to be completed.

"Who" refers to people, and "that" refers to things.

The time should be written as "5:00."

"Every" and "neighbors" are the correct spellings.

Names of days of the week are capitalized.

A Sentence a Day

Fragments, word choice, spelling, capitalization

Paula was so proud of her newest invenshun a glow in the dark plunger.

Paula was so proud of her newest invention: a glow-in-the-dark plunger.

"Invention" is the correct spelling.

The first part of the sentence "announces" something—a perfect opportunity for a colon. A dash would also work, and so would a comma.

Hyphens in compound adjectives signal to the reader that the adjectives ("glow-in-the-dark") all refer to the noun that follows: "plunger."

Steves' stomach reminded him that judgeing the chili cook-off, and participating in the catamaran race, on the same day, was not a good plan.

Steve's stomach reminded him that judging the chili cook-off and participating in the catamaran race on the same day was not a good plan.

"Steve's" should have an apostrophe before the *s*, not after. (Putting it after the *s* would indicate more than one Steve.)

"Judging" has no *e*. Many words drop the final *e* when adding "ing."

The writer has gone a bit comma crazy on this one. Actually, no commas at all are necessary.

Sometimes you have to do things you don't want to do, the father reminded his son as they put on candy cane hats and waited for their cue to appeer on stage.

"Sometimes you have to do things you don't want to do," the father reminded his son as they put on candy cane hats and waited for their cue to appear on stage.

Because the father's exact words are used, they should be enclosed in quotation marks.

"Appear" is the correct spelling.

A comma is acceptable after "sometimes," though it isn't necessary.

A Sentence a Day

incorrect

Flora smiled, and introduced her too plants as Phil and Rhoda Dendron.

correct

Flora smiled and introduced her two plants as Phil and Rhoda Dendron.

notes

There is no need to use a comma between the two parts of a compound verb (smiled and introduced).

"Two" is the word to use when expressing a number.

Whom *does* like green eggs and ham, I sertainly do'nt, I do'nt even like green things that are *suppose* to be green.

Who *does* like green eggs and ham? I certainly don't. I don't even like green things that are *supposed* to be green.

The correct word needed here is "who," not "whom." Substitute "he," "she," or "they" for "who" or "whom." If it sounds correct, use "who." Then substitute "him," "her," or "them" for "who" or "whom." If it sounds correct, use "whom." In this example, substitute "he" for "whom": "He does like green eggs and ham." That sounds correct, so you would use "who." Then substitute "him" for "whom": "Him does like green eggs and ham." That sounds incorrect, so you wouldn't use "whom."

The item is a comma splice, a type of run-on sentence. The first part is a question and needs a question mark. A period is needed after "I certainly don't." Or use a semicolon or a conjunction. Some conjunctions don't necessarily require a comma ("because," "if," "though," "since"). Others do require a comma, such as coordinating conjunctions ("for," "and," "nor," "but," "or," "yet," "so," or FANBOYS).

"Certainly" is the correct spelling.

"Don't" is the correct spelling. The apostrophe goes between the *n* and the *t*, to represent the *o* that is left out of "not."

Though it may sound like "suppose to" when someone says it, the phrase is really "supposed to," with a *d*.

Word choice, run-ons,
spelling, apostrophes

A Sentence a Day

Diegos dream was to launch his homemade drone from the top of the eiffel tower in paris. Or at least from the top of duke's plumbing supply in paris, texas.

Diego's dream was to launch his homemade drone from the top of the Eiffel Tower in Paris, or at least from the top of Duke's Plumbing Supply in Paris, Texas.

The dream "belongs" to Diego. Therefore, "Diego's" is possessive and needs an apostrophe.

"Eiffel Tower" is the name of a certain structure, so it is capitalized, as is "Paris," the name of a city.

Duke's Plumbing Supply is the name of a store, so it should be capitalized.

"Or at least from the top of Duke's Plumbing Supply" is a sentence fragment. It should be part of the previous sentence, separated by a comma or a dash.

A Sentence a Day

Apostrophes, capitalization, fragments

Because the students names came over the intercom in a voice that definately didn't sound very happy.

Because the students' names came over the intercom in a voice that definitely didn't sound very happy, the students weren't exactly eager to report to the office.

The names belong to more than one student. Therefore, the apostrophe goes *after* the *s*.

The item is a sentence fragment that needs to be completed.

"Definitely" definitely does not have an *a* in it.

The classroom hamster was a fussy little thing the students' tried to feed it lettuce but it wouldn't eat anything except chunks of left-over bean burritoes.

The classroom hamster was a fussy little thing. The students tried to feed it lettuce, but it wouldn't eat anything except chunks of leftover bean burritos.

Because "students" is not a possessive here, it needs no apostrophe.

The item is a run-on sentence. A period, semicolon, or conjunction is needed after "thing."

A comma is needed after lettuce since "The students tried to feed it lettuce, but it wouldn't eat anything except chunks of bean burritos" is a compound sentence. A compound sentence requires a comma along with a coordinating conjunction (FANBOYS: "for," "and," "nor," "but," "or," "yet," "so").

There is no *e* in "burritos."

A Sentence a Day

Apostrophes, run-ons, spelling

Dee desided to quit her job at dottie's dairy delight because the double chocolate mocha malts were delighting her a little to much, she had gained ten lbs. since starting the job only a Month ago.

Dee decided to quit her job at Dottie's Dairy Delight because the double chocolate mocha malts were delighting her a little too much. She had gained ten pounds since starting the job only a month ago.

"Decided" has no *s* in it.

"Dottie's Dairy Delight" should be capitalized because it is the name of a certain store.

The malts delighted Dee "too" much. "Too" is used to mean "very."

Except in very informal writing or in lists, "pounds" should be written out, not abbreviated as "lbs."

Names of months are capitalized, but the word "month" is not.

The comma between "much" and "she" should be replaced with a period, a semicolon, or a conjunction to eliminate the comma splice, which is a type of run-on sentence.

Balancing a birthday cake with flaming candles on his head Travis was the life some would say "light" of the party.

Balancing a birthday cake with flaming candles on his head, Travis was the life—some would say "light"—of the party.

"Balancing a birthday cake with flaming candles on his head" is an introductory element (a phrase). It should be followed by a comma.

"Some would say 'light'" is an aside, an interruption. It should be set off with dashes or put in parentheses.

A Sentence a Day

Commas,
dashes

Frank a chimpanzee was totaly in love with gladys a aardvark.

Frank, a chimpanzee, was totally in love with Gladys, an aard-vark.

The sentence contains two appositives that should be set off with commas: "a chimpanzee" and "an aardvark."

"Totally" has two *l*'s.

"Gladys" is capitalized because it is a proper noun.

"An" is used before words that begin with a vowel sound.

The alien the one who had traveled 27 light-years to reach planet earth was dissapointed to find that the coffee shop he had wanted to visit for 20 light-years was out of expresso.

The alien, the one who had traveled 27 light-years to reach planet Earth, was disappointed to find that the coffee shop he had wanted to visit for 20 light-years was out of espresso.

"The one who had traveled 27 light-years to reach the Earth" is an interrupting element (an appositive) that should be set off with commas.

"Earth" is the name of a planet in this sentence and therefore should be capitalized.

"Disappointed" has one *s* and two *p*'s.

Though many people pronounce it "expresso," the word is really "espresso."

A Sentence a Day

Commas, capitalization, spelling, apostrophes

"When you say your going to die if you have to go to school on a bair hair day I think your exaggerating just a bit" said Jennifers mother.

"When you say you're going to die if you have to go to school on a bad hair day, I think you're exaggerating just a bit," said Jennifer's mother.

"You're" is the correct word to use when "you are" can be substituted in the sentence.

"When you say you're going to die if you have to go to school on a bad hair day" is an introductory element (a clause). It should be separated from the rest of the sentence with a comma.

There should be a comma after "bit," to separate the words in the direct quotation from the dialogue tag, "said Jennifer's mother."

The mother "belongs" to Jennifer. "Jennifer's" needs an apostrophe to show possession.

Orin's grandmother just couldn't beleive he didn't like cute stuffed teddy bears alphabet blocks and his tricycle anymore, even though he was about to graduate from high school.

Orin's grandmother just couldn't believe he didn't like cute stuffed teddy bears, alphabet blocks(,) and his tricycle anymore, even though he was about to graduate from high school.

Items in a series should be separated by commas. The comma before "or" is optional.

"Believe" follows the "*i* before *e* except after *c*" rule.

Casey likes new england clam chowder, but his dad, he prefers manhattan clam chowder, his sister, though, gets queasy even thinking about clam chowder.

Casey likes New England clam chowder, but his dad prefers Manhattan clam chowder. His sister, though, gets queasy even thinking about clam chowder.

"New England" and "Manhattan" are capitalized because they are the names of specific places.

"His dad, he" is a double subject. There is no need for the "he" or the comma after "dad."

The item is a comma splice, a type of run-on sentence. Two complete sentences cannot be separated by a comma. Add a period, a semicolon, or a conjunction after "Manhattan clam chowder." Some conjunctions don't necessarily require a comma ("because," "if," "though," "since"). Others do require a comma, such as coordinating conjunctions ("for," "and," "nor," "but," "or," "yet," "so," or FANBOYS).

A Sentence a Day

Isadora looked at the picture of prairie chickens in her science book and wondered, "are there also forest chickens, swamp chickens, and mountain chickens.

Isadora looked at the picture of prairie chickens in her science book and wondered, "Are there also forest chickens, swamp chickens(,) and mountain chickens?"

The first word of a sentence in a quotation should be capitalized. Therefore, "are" should be capitalized.

The sentence in quotation marks is a question, so it should end in a question mark.

Quotation marks always come in pairs. They occur at the beginning *and* at the end of a quotation.

Items in a series should be separated by commas. The comma before "and" is optional.

A Sentence a Day

Capitalization, question marks, quotation marks, commas

Henry looked at his grown son sighed and said, do you have any life goals besides trying to acquire the largest tv known to humankind?

Henry looked at his grown son, sighed(,) and said, "Do you have any life goals besides trying to acquire the largest TV known to humankind?"

Items in a series should be separated by commas. The comma before the final "and" is optional.

A direct quotation should be enclosed in quotation marks.

The first word of a sentence in a quotation should be capitalized.

The acronym for "television" is capitalized: "TV."

Jeremiah glared at the girls laughing at him. "Well *you* try riding a bicicle while you're wearing giant plastic duck feet" he yelled!

Jeremiah glared at the girls laughing at him. "Well, *you* try riding a bicycle while you're wearing giant plastic duck feet!" he yelled.

Introductory words such as "yes," "no," "oh," and "well" should be followed by a comma.

"Bicycle" has only one *i*.

The exclamation point belongs after Jeremiah's words, not after "he yelled."

A Sentence a Day

Commas, spelling, exclamation points

Madeline didn't like the spam that came with her e-mail, the spam that her Grandma always fried up with eggs in the morning, or spamalot, the Broadway musical.

Madeline didn't like the spam that came with her email, the Spam that her grandma always fried up with eggs in the morning, or *Spamalot*, the Broadway musical.

"Spam" is used in two different ways. The Spam that comes in a can is capitalized because it is a brand name. The other kind of spam is not.

According to the dictionary, "e-mail" or "email" are acceptable spellings. Currently, "email" without a hyphen seems to be the preferred spelling. Use one or the other consistently.

"Grandma" is not capitalized unless it's being used as a name: "We love Grandma."

"*Spamalot*" is capitalized and italicized because it is the name of a musical.

Items in a series should be separated by commas. The final comma is optional.

Clarissa loves the music of the green electrodes, her Father on the other hand does not.

Clarissa loves the music of the Green Electrodes, but her father, on the other hand, does not.

The name of the band should be capitalized.

Unless it's being used as a name, "father" is not capitalized.

The item is a run-on sentence. One option is to add a coordinating conjunction after the comma.

Parenthetical expressions like "on the other hand," "by the way," and "in my opinion" should be set off with commas.

A Sentence a Day

Capitalization, run-ons, commas

little Salvadors uncle from jackson wyoming told him he was coming to see him and bringing along his pet moose.

Little Salvador's uncle from Jackson, Wyoming, told him he was coming to see him and bringing along his pet moose.

"Little" should be capitalized, since it is the beginning of the sentence.

"Salvador's" needs an apostrophe. The uncle "belongs" to Salvador.

"Jackson" and "Wyoming" should be capitalized.

A comma should be placed after "Jackson" and after "Wyoming." (Most people remember the comma between the city and state. A comma should also be used after the state.)

As the secret hatch slowly creaked open and a blew tentacle uncoiled from the darkness.

As the secret hatch slowly creaked open and a blue tentacle uncoiled from the darkness, Timothy decided it was time to go.

"Blue" is the word to use when referring to a color. "Blew" is what the wind did yesterday.

The item is a sentence fragment that needs to be completed. What happened as the secret hatch opened and the tentacle uncoiled?

A Sentence a Day

Word choice,
fragments

Mark stood in front of his teacher, and said "Miss Nordlestorp I know you won't beleive me but my dog ate not only my homework but also my Game Boy and a pair of my socks."

Mark stood in front of his teacher and said, "Miss Nordlestorp, I know you won't believe me, but my dog ate not only my homework but also my Game Boy and a pair of my socks."

There is no need for a comma after "teacher." A comma *is* needed after "said."

Mark is directly addressing Miss Nordlestorp, so a comma is needed after her name.

"Believe" follows the "*i* before *e* except after *c*" rule.

"I know you won't believe me, but my dog ate . . ." is a compound sentence. A comma is used before the coordinating conjunction in a compound sentence. (No comma is needed in "not only my homework but also my Game Boy" because there "but" is not acting as a conjunction separating two complete sentences.)

Learn how to play the kazoo Charlie, or your out of the band.

Learn how to play the kazoo, Charlie, or you're out of the band.

"Charlie" is being directly addressed, so his name should be set off with commas.

"You're" is the word needed.

Commas,
word choice

The hover car zoomed across the hot dessert, carrying the accordianists to their sold-out concert in las vegas.

The hover car zoomed across the hot desert, carrying the accordionists to their sold-out concert in Las Vegas.

The accordionists were not, presumably, zooming across a dish of hot apple cobbler. Therefore, the word needed is "desert," not "dessert."

"Accordionists" has only one *a*, the first one. (Perhaps not everyone needs to know that "accordion" doesn't end in "an." What is important is that students know to check the spelling of any word that is the least bit unfamiliar.)

Names of cities should be capitalized.

Why would anyone ever want to become a dentist wondered rochelle. I can't imagine spending my life looking at peoples teeth and gums. Me, neither, said Cooper. I'd much rather be a podia-trist and look at peoples feet.

"Why would anyone ever want to become a dentist?" wondered Rochelle. "I can't imagine spending my life looking at people's teeth and gums."

"Me, neither," said Cooper. "I'd much rather be a podiatrist and look at people's feet."

In dialogue, a new paragraph begins with each change of speakers.

A question mark is needed after "Why would anyone ever want to become a dentist?"

Quotation marks should be used around the exact words spoken by a character.

"People's" should have an apostrophe before the *s*. The teeth "belong" to people.

A Sentence a Day

Dialogue, question marks,
quotation marks, apostrophes

Little Nathaniel looked up at his angry mother and said, "A rabbit came into my room and said, Don't listen to anything your Mother says. He seemed like a smart rabbit, so I desided to do what he said."

Little Nathaniel looked up at his angry mother and said, "A rabbit came into my room and said, 'Don't listen to anything your mother says.' He seemed like a smart rabbit, so I decided to do what he said."

Neither use of "mother" should be capitalized. "Mother" should be capitalized only when it is used as a person's name.

"Decided" is the correct spelling.

Nathaniel is being quoted, and he in turn is quoting the rabbit. What Nathaniel says should be placed inside double quotation marks. What the rabbit says should be placed inside single quotation marks. (Students may be interested to know that the British do it in exactly the opposite way. They use single quotes around a quotation, with double quotes for a quotation within a quotation.)

Capitalization, spelling, quotation marks

A Sentence a Day

I love tempeh more then just about anything in the world, except maybe for Emma Sue Taguchi." said Craig. "Tempeh is alot more loveable then Emma Sue Taguchi in my opinion" said John.

"I love tempeh more than just about anything else in the world, except maybe for Emma Sue Taguchi," said Craig.

"Tempeh is a lot more loveable than Emma Sue Taguchi, in my opinion," said John.

"Than" is the correct word in this sentence because it refers to a comparison between tempeh and anything and tempeh and Emma Sue Taguchi. "Then" refers to time/order or means "in that case," "as a necessary consequence," "besides," and some other similar things. "Upon arrival, I knew I had a better costume than anyone else at the party, and then I won the costume contest."

In dialogue, a new paragraph begins with each change of speakers.

A comma should separate the quotation from dialogue tags like "he said."

"A lot" is two words, not one.

Parenthetical expressions such as "on the other hand," "as a matter of fact," and "in my opinion" should be set off with commas.

A Sentence a Day

Dialogue, spelling, commas

To buoys and to grills went two see the amazing chihuahuas play volleyball but they're patients ran out when they had too weight so long for a ticket.

Two boys and two girls went to see the Amazing Chihuahuas play volleyball, but their patience ran out when they had to wait so long for a ticket.

This sentence is a perfect illustration of the limits of spell-check programs. Spell-check would find nothing wrong with the sentence when, in fact, there are many errors: "Two boys" and "two girls," "to" see, "their patience," and "to wait."

Because the sentence is a compound sentence (two complete sentences connected with "but"), a comma is needed before "but." Compound sentences are punctuated with a comma *and* a coordinating conjunction ("for," "and," "nor," "but," "or," "yet," "so," or FANBOYS).

Should it be "there," "they're," or "their"? "Their" is the word used to show possession.

"Amazing Chihuahuas" should be capitalized because it's the name of the volleyball team. "Chihuahua" is always capitalized as a proper noun because it's the name of a state in Mexico.

The frist thing Eric did after he looked out his window and saw the ostrich standing beside the diving bored of the swimming pool.

The first thing Eric did after he looked out his window and saw the ostrich standing beside the diving board of the swimming pool was grab his digital camera and take a picture.

The item is a sentence fragment and needs to be completed. *What* was the first thing Eric did?

"First" is the correct spelling.

The ostrich was standing beside the diving "board," not "bored." (The ostrich might have been "bored," but we don't know that from the sentence.)

A Sentence a Day

Fragments, spelling, word choice

My freind visited yesterday and he looks at my room and goes, "Don't you find black walls kinda depressing."

My friend visited yesterday, and he looked at my room and said, "Don't you find black walls kind of depressing?"

"Friend" follows the "*i* before *e* except after *c*" rule.

Because the item is a compound sentence, a comma should be placed before "and."

The sentence starts out in past tense ("visited"), so it should not switch to present tense ("looks").

The friend didn't "go." He "said."

"Kinda" should be written "kind of."

The friend asked a question, so the quotation should end in a question mark.

Egbert use to say he liked eggplant, but then he tasted it, and changed his mind.

Egbert used to say he liked eggplant, but then he tasted it and changed his mind.

"Use to" should be "used to."

There is no need for a comma between compound verbs ("tasted" and "changed").

Brad is flying to england in the Fall to visit museums with his Grandfather, but what he is really looking forward to is flying to hawaii next July to serf with his Brother.

Brad is flying to England in the fall to visit museums with his grandfather, but what he is really looking forward to is flying to Hawaii next July to surf with his brother.

"England" and "Hawaii" are the names of specific places, so they should be capitalized.

Months of the year are capitalized, but seasons are not.

"Grandfather" should be capitalized only when it is being used as a person's name, as in, "Will you go with me, Grandfather?"

"Surf" is the word to use for what a person might do in Hawaii. "Serf" refers to a kind of slave.

"Brother" should not be capitalized since it is not a specific name.

Noone knows why elwood showed up covered in bean dip and looking angry, everyone was afraid to ask though.

No one knows why Elwood showed up covered in bean dip and looking angry. Everyone was afraid to ask, though.

"No one" is two words.

"Elwood" is a proper noun and should be capitalized.

The item is a comma splice, a type of run-on sentence. A comma cannot be used to separate two complete sentences. Therefore, a period, a semicolon, or a conjunction should replace the comma after "angry." Some conjunctions don't necessarily require a comma ("because," "if," "though," "since"). Others do require a comma, such as coordinating conjunctions ("for," "and," "nor," "but," "or," "yet," "so," or FANBOYS).

When "though" is used as an adverb, usually at the end of a sentence, use a comma before it.

A Sentence a Day

Spelling, capitalization, run-ons, commas

Wear in the world did you put my gold chicken statute at.

Where in the world did you put my gold chicken statue?

"Where" and "statue" are the correct spellings.

Because the sentence is a question, it should end in a question mark.

"At" is completely unnecessary at the end of the sentence.

Miss Edwards the first grade teacher at fernwood elementary school was trying to be kind when she told Chandlers parents that he was a very exuberant child who loved experimenting with language, what she meant was that he was wild and used bad words.

Miss Edwards, the first-grade teacher at Fernwood Elementary School, was trying to be kind when she told Chandler's parents that he was a very exuberant child who loved experimenting with language, but what she meant was that he was wild and used bad words.

"The first-grade teacher at Fernwood Elementary School" is an interrupting element (an appositive) that should be set off with commas.

Hyphens in compound adjectives signal to the reader that the adjectives ("first-grade") all refer to the noun that follows: "teacher."

"Fernwood Elementary School" should be capitalized.

"Chandler's" should have an apostrophe before the *s*. The parents "belong" to Chandler.

The item is a comma splice, a type of run-on sentence. One option is to add a conjunction between "language" and "what." Or use a semicolon or a period. Some conjunctions don't necessarily require a comma ("because," "if," "though," "since"). Others do require a comma, such as coordinating conjunctions ("for," "and," "nor," "but," "or," "yet," "so," or FANBOYS).

A Sentence a Day

Commas, hyphens, capitalization, apostrophes, run-ons

"I hate frogs even more then I hate licorice" exclaimed little Ashley when Charlie presented her with one during reesess.

"I hate frogs even more than I hate licorice!" exclaimed little Ashley when Charlie presented her with one during recess.

"Than" is the correct word in this sentence because it refers to a comparison between frogs and licorice. "Then" refers to time/order or means "in that case," "as a necessary consequence," "besides," and some other similar things. "Upon arrival, I knew I had a better costume than anyone else at the party, and then I won the costume contest."

Since Ashley "exclaimed," the quotation should have an exclamation point after it.

"Recess" is the correct spelling.

When there knew kitten started scratching olive the furniture, the Peterson family got pretty flustrated and regretted they're decision to get a kitten instead of an aquarium full of fish.

When their new kitten started scratching all of the furniture, the Peterson family got pretty frustrated and regretted their decision to get a kitten instead of an aquarium full of fish.

The sentence has many spelling/word choice errors, all corrected above. Interestingly, many people incorrectly use "flustrated," instead of "frustrated." One theory is that they are confusing "flustered" and "frustrated."

A Sentence a Day

Spelling, word choice

Shalana had waited months to see Evil Crawdads Three but she wasn't too pleased with the plotholes that were like pot holes jolting her out of the story every ten minutes.

Shalana had waited months to see *Evil Crawdads 3*, but she wasn't too pleased with the plot holes that were like potholes jolting her out of the story every ten minutes.

A comma is required before a coordinating conjunction ("for," "and," "nor," "but," "or," "yet," "so," or FANBOYS).

Movie titles are italicized: *Evil Crawdads 3*.

Movie sequel numbers are written as numerals, not spelled out. "Three" in the movie title is the sequel number, so it should be written as "3." Movie sequels also use Roman numerals: *Jurassic Park III*, for example.

"Plot holes" is two words.

"Potholes" is one word.

At the end of the day after the dust settled the influencers which included Danger Bike Ike influenced their parents to limit phone time starting according to Ikes' Mom immediately.

After their parents saw their posts and scolded them for their behavior, the influencers, which included Danger Bike Ike, influenced their parents to limit phone time starting, according to Ike's mom, immediately.

Introductory and parenthetical commas make the sentence easier to read.

"At the end of the day" and "after the dust settled" are clichés. Watch for these overused phrases and replace them with specific descriptions.

"Mom" is not capitalized unless it's being used in place of a person's name. "Please, Mom, don't limit my phone time."

"Ike's" is correct because there is only one Ike in the sentence, and apostrophe "s" indicates there is one possessive noun.

A Sentence a Day

Apostrophes, capitalization, clichés, commas

Yesterday Wakeisha wondered if a Water Bear would make a good pet and asks her parents to buy her one.

Yesterday, Wakeisha wondered if a water bear would make a good pet and asked her parents to buy her one.

Add a comma after "yesterday," which is an introductory element in this sentence.

The term "water bear" is a common noun and should not be capitalized. But if Wakeisha uses the term as a name, it would be capitalized: "Wakeisha named her dog Water Bear."

The sentence uses the past tense verb "wondered" and the present tense verb "asks," which is incorrect because we know both things occurred yesterday, which is in the past.

Bina was sure the bug named zombee face in the youtube video everyone was talking about was not an actual Zombee.

Bina was sure the bug named Zombie Face in the YouTube video everyone was talking about was not an actual zombie.

"Zombie" is the correct spelling, not "zombee." However, who's to say "zombee" isn't how the actual name is spelled? People who post things online have been known to misspell words. Ideally, you want to check the spellings of names and record them as is, no matter how badly they are spelled.

"Zombie Face" or "Zombee Face" should be capitalized because it's a name and therefore a proper noun.

"YouTube" is the correct spelling. Bicapitalization is capitalizing a letter in the middle of a word or name. Have students write down other examples of company names that use bicapitalization.

"Everyone" is the correct spelling.

The last word of the sentence is spelled "zombie." It's a common noun and is not capitalized.

Oscar, he imagined an orange and a tanjereen and wondered which was more oranger.

Oscar imagined an orange and a tangerine and wondered which was oranger.

"Oscar, he" is a double subject. There is no need to say "he."

"Tangerine" is the correct spelling.

The three forms of the adjective "orange" are "orange" (to describe one thing), "oranger" (to compare two things), and "orangest" (to compare three things.) "More" is unnecessary with "oranger."

Rajiv tells his sister to hurry up, and win the videogame but she says "than I won't wanna play it any more.

Rajiv tells his sister to hurry up and win the video game, but she says, "then I won't want to play it anymore."

No comma is needed after "up" because "and win the videogame" is part of the first clause before "but."

A comma is needed before "but" because it's a coordinating conjunction ("for," "and," "nor," "but," "or," "yet," "so," or FANBOYS).

A comma is required after "says" because a quote follows.

The correct spelling is "video game."

"Then" is the correct word in this sentence because it refers to time/order. "Then" also means "in that case," "as a necessary consequence," "besides," and some other similar things. "Than" is used when comparing things.

"Wanna" should be "want to" and "any more" should be "anymore." Ask students to read the definitions of "any more" and "anymore" and explain the difference.

A Sentence a Day

Commas, spelling, word choice

Joe was to busy to go to blobfest at the colonial theatre because he had to attend a zoom, and then watch a tick tock.

Joe was too busy to go to Blobfest at the Colonial Theatre because he had to attend a Zoom and then watch a TikTok.

Joe was "too" busy. "Too" is used to express a degree of something, as in "too much ice cream."

"Blobfest," "Colonial Theatre," "Zoom," and "TikTok" are proper nouns, so they should be capitalized. "TikTok" happens to spell its name with the second T capitalized as well.

No comma is needed after "Zoom" because "then watch a TikTok" is a dependent clause.

Kayshon wanted to know, if there was a armacy to go with an legasy.

Kayshon wanted to know if there was an "armacy" to go with a legacy.

There is no need for a comma after "know."

"A" is used before words beginning with a consonant sound. "An" is used before words beginning with a vowel sound.

"Legacy" is the correct spelling.

Double quotation marks should be used around made-up words to avoid confusion.

Although the ghosts lived in the same house for over 500 years the ghosts desided to move, cuz the new family had a daily habit of playing dish drain jenga.

Although the ghosts lived in the same house for over 500 years, they decided to move because the new family had a daily habit of playing dish drain Jenga.

A comma is needed after the introductory phrase that begins with "although" and ends with "years."

Instead of repeating the noun "ghosts," use the pronoun "they."

The correct spellings are "decided" and "because."

The comma before "because" is not needed.

"Jenga" is a proper noun, so it should be capitalized.

To much time on Social Media literally turned her mind into a junkdrawer, that needed to be cleaned out.

Too much time on social media turned her mind into a junk drawer that needed to be cleaned out.

"Too" is the word to use, not "to." "Too" is used to express a degree of something, as in "too much ice cream." "Too" can also be used to mean "also."

There is no need to capitalize "social media" because it's a common noun.

Regarding "literally," did her mind actually become a junk drawer? Probably not. If you're being metaphorical, leave out "literally" and use a simile ("Her mind was like a junk drawer that needed to be cleaned out.") or a metaphor ("Her mind was a junk drawer that needed to be cleaned out.")

"Junk drawer" is two words.

The sentence does not require a comma.

A Sentence a Day

Word choice, capitalization, commas

Snap Chat is used by most of the teen-agers in Boring, OR.

Most of the teenagers in Boring, Oregon, use Snapchat.

Active voice means someone or something does something. Passive voice means someone or something has something done to them. Passive voice always uses a "to be" verb (for example, "was" or "were"). For the most part, you want to use active voice in formal writing, but passive voice has its place as well. Usually, you can fix passive voice by putting the subject before the verb and changing the "to be" verb.

"Snapchat" and "teenagers" are the correct spellings.

Generally, postal abbreviations of states should be confined to envelopes and lists. It's usually best to spell out the state when writing sentences.

In the corrected item, note that a comma should be placed after "Boring" and after "Oregon." (Most people remember the comma between the city and state. A comma should also be used after the state, abbreviated or not.)

Passive voice, spelling,
abbreviations, commas

A Sentence a Day

Ezra planted the supreme pizza plant that he bought on amazon but when it grew he discovered it was a canadian bacon and pine apple plant.

Ezra planted the supreme pizza plant that he bought on Amazon, but when it grew, he discovered it was a Canadian bacon and pineapple plant.

We don't know if "supreme pizza plant" is the name of the plant. If it is, it should be capitalized: "Supreme Pizza Plant."

"Amazon" is a proper noun and should be capitalized.

A comma is required after "Amazon" because "but" is a coordinating conjunction.

A comma is required after "grew" because "when it grew" is an introductory phrase.

"Canadian" is a proper noun, so it is capitalized.

"Pineapple" is one word.

We don't know if "Canadian bacon and pineapple plant" is the name of the plant. If it is, it should be capitalized: "Canadian Bacon and Pineapple Plant."

A Sentence a Day

Capitalization, commas, spelling

Basically at that point in time I was of the opinion that I was sort of to tired too go to bed.

I was too tired to go to bed.

Eliminate wordiness by deleting words and phrases such as "basically," "at that point in time," "I was of the opinion," and "sort of."

"To" is the word to use, not "too." "Too" is used to express a degree of something, as in "too much ice cream."

She paints her lawn with a sherwin-williams color called fabulous grape, she thinks green is unbearibly boaring.

She paints her lawn with a Sherwin-Williams color called Fabulous Grape because she thinks green is unbearably boring.

"Sherwin-Williams" and "Fabulous Grape" should be capitalized because they are names and therefore proper nouns.

The item is a comma splice, a type of run-on sentence. Two complete sentences cannot be separated by a comma. Use a semicolon, a period, or a conjunction. Some conjunctions don't necessarily require a comma ("because," "if," "though," "since"). Others do require a comma, such as coordinating conjunctions ("for," "and," "nor," "but," "or," "yet," "so," or FANBOYS).

The correct spellings are "unbearably" and "boring."

Her best avatar are Clown Bunny, her other creashuns is also impressive, Cowboy Octupus, Doctor Dingo, and Queen Cheesecake.

Her best avatar is Clown Bunny, but her other creations are also impressive: Cowboy Octopus, Doctor Dingo, and Queen Cheesecake.

The item is a comma splice, a type of run-on sentence. One option is to add a coordinating conjunction after the comma. Or use a semicolon or a period. Some conjunctions don't necessarily require a comma ("because," "if," "though," "since"). Others do require a comma, such as coordinating conjunctions ("for," "and," "nor," "but," "or," "yet," "so," or FANBOYS).

Her best avatar is "Clown Bunny"—only one—so the verb "are" should be changed to "is" to agree with "avatar." In the second part of the sentence, there are "creations"—more than one—so the verb "is" should be changed to "are."

"Creations" and "octopus" are the correct spellings.

Use a colon to introduce a list.

The brothers didn't want to go to egg land the amusment park in their home town of chicken, Alaska because the brothers were bored with the roaring rooster coaster, the egg salad scrambler, and the big bantam bumper cars.

The brothers didn't want to go to Egg Land, the amusement park in their hometown of Chicken, Alaska, because they were bored with the Roaring Rooster Coaster, the Egg Salad Scrambler, and the Big Bantam Bumper Cars.

"The amusement park in their hometown of Chicken, Alaska" is an appositive that gives more information about Egg Land. It interrupts the flow of the sentence and should be set off with commas.

The correct capitalizations are "Egg Land," "Chicken," "Alaska," "Roaring Rooster Coaster," "Egg Salad Scrambler," and "Big Bantam Bumper Cars."

"Amusement" and "hometown" are the correct spellings.

Instead of repeating the noun "brothers," use the pronoun "they."

A Sentence a Day

Commas, spelling, capitalization, pronouns

Lets let the luvly Lizards lerking in the lavendar Lylacks lazily lownge on our loominus Laptop.

Let's let the lovely lizards lurking in the lavender lilacs lazily lounge on our luminous laptop.

"Let's" is a contraction for "let us." "Lets" means to allow or permit, among other things.

The correct spellings are "lovely," "lurking," "lavender," "lilacs," "lounge," "luminous," and "laptop."

"Lizards," "lilacs," and "laptop" are common nouns and should not be capitalized.

The cutest gif features baby goats wearing santa clause pajama's.

The cutest GIF features baby goats wearing Santa Claus pajamas.

Each letter in "GIF" is capitalized because it is the acronym for "graphic interchange format." The rule for acronyms in formal writing when referring to them times is to spell out the words of the acronym the first time you use it and put the capitalized letters for the acronym in parentheses behind the mention. In subsequent referrals, use the capitalized letters for the acronym. This is not necessary for familiar acronyms (FBI, NASA). If you're only referring to the acronym once, spell it out.

"Santa Claus" is capitalized because it's a proper noun.

The correct spelling is "claus," not "clause."

There is no need for an apostrophe in "pajamas."

Zara's self driving car princess zoom zoom has it's own facebook page, and it has more friends than I do.

Zara's self-driving car, Princess Zoom Zoom, has its own Facebook page, and it has more friends than I do.

Most "self" compounds are hyphenated: "self-driving." Other examples include "self-confidence," "self-esteem," "self-reflection," "self-examination."

"Princess Zoom Zoom" is an appositive. It interrupts the flow of the sentence to give more information about "car" and should be set off with commas.

"Its" is a pronoun used to show ownership or possession. There is no apostrophe in it.

"Facebook" is a proper noun, so it should be capitalized. "Princess Zoom Zoom" is the name of Zara's car, so it should be capitalized.

Last year, the class asks artificial intelligence to compare apples' to apples' and they broke the internet cuz their are 7500 apple varieties through out the world.

Last year, the class asked artificial intelligence to compare apples to apples, and they broke the internet because there are 7,500 apple varieties throughout the world.

The item above switches tenses. It starts out with a verb in present tense ("asks") and switches to past tense ("broke"). If the class did something "last year," that was in the past, so the verb "ask" should be past tense: "asked." Now, students may wonder why the verb "are" is correct because it is in present tense and the other verbs in the sentence are in past tense. Have them explore why that is. An example would be if more varieties of apples were discovered or invented and added to the total. Then it would be "there *were* 7,500 apple varieties. Now there *are* 7,501."

"Apples" is a plural noun here and is not possessive, so no apostrophe is needed.

A comma is needed after the second "apples" because a comma is required before a coordinating conjunction ("for," "and," "nor," "but," "or," "yet," "so," or FANBOYS).

There are several spelling mistakes in this sentence. "Cuz" should be "because," "their" should be "there," and "through out" should be "throughout."

For numbers with four or more digits, a comma goes after the first digit: "7,500."

A Sentence a Day

Verb tense, apostrophes,
commas, spelling

My Uncle lives in a luxurius camper in the wilderness he can't always get internet acsess, therefore, he prefers vhs over Streaming.

My uncle lives in a luxurious camper in the wilderness, but he can't always get Internet access; therefore, he prefers VHS over streaming.

"Uncle" is not capitalized when it's preceded by a pronoun such as "your" or "my." However, if "Uncle" is used as a person's name, it is capitalized.

"Internet" is capitalized, according to the dictionary, but "internet," lowercase, is becoming more popular.

It should be "streaming," lowercase, because it is a common noun.

The sentence contains a run-on. Use a semicolon or a period between "wilderness" and "he."

The correct spellings are "luxurious" and "access."

The second part of the sentence after "access" is a comma splice, a type of run-on sentence. A comma cannot separate two sentences. Use a semicolon or a period between "access" and "therefore."

"VHS" is an acronym for "Video Home System," so each letter is capitalized. To be more precise, this example of an acronym is an initialism. An initialism is an acronym where each letter is read as a letter (ATM, DVD) instead of combining the letters into a new word (GIF, BOGO). "VHS" cannot really be pronounced in a way that makes sense, so it is an initialism.

The rule for acronyms in formal writing when referring to them multiple times is to spell out the words of the acronym the first time you use it and put the capitalized letters for the acronym in parentheses behind the mention. In subsequent referrals, use the capitalized letters for the acronym. This is not necessary for familiar acronyms (FBI, NASA). If you're only referring to the acronym once, spell it out.

They had misgivings about the hungry jack mash potatoes challenge, however, they went a head with it any way and will never eat mash potatoes again.

They had misgivings about the Hungry Jack Mashed Potatoes Challenge; however, they went ahead with it anyway and will never eat mashed potatoes again.

"Hungry Jack Mashed Potatoes" is a brand name's specific product, so it should be capitalized. "Challenge" should be capitalized because it is part of the name of the specific challenge title. If you were referring in general to "internet challenges," for example, "challenges" would not be capitalized.

The item is a comma splice, a type of run-on sentence. A comma cannot separate two sentences. Use a semicolon or a period between "challenge" and "however."

The correct spellings are "mashed," "ahead," and "anyway."

Lucia refuses to hire any one for her band who does'nt know how to play: the Hurdy-gurdy, Didgeridoo, Theremin, Theorbo, Cimbalon and Zurna.

Lucia refuses to hire anyone for her band who doesn't know how to play the hurdy-gurdy, didgeridoo, theremin, theorbo, cimbalon, and zurna.

"Anyone" and "doesn't" are the correct spellings.

No colon is needed after "play." To use a colon, the part of the sentence before the colon should really be a sentence itself. Here is an example:

Lucia requires her band members to play some strange instruments you've probably never heard of: the hurdy-gurdy, didgeridoo, theremin, theorbo, cimbalon, and zurna.

The names of the instruments are common nouns and are not capitalized.

You might want to include a comma before "and" to make it clear that "cimbalon" and "zurna" are two separate instruments.

After he seen the meen meem he said a meem can be meen, you know what I meen.

After he saw the mean meme, he said, "A meme can be mean. You know what I mean?"

The correct verb form here is "saw." "Seen" always needs a helping verb before it—he *has* seen, he *will have* seen, he *was* seen, he *will be* seen, etc.

"Mean" and "meme" are the correct spellings.

"After he saw the mean meme" is an introductory element and should be followed by a comma.

The quote has a comma splice, a type of run-on sentence. A comma cannot be used alone to separate two sentences. A period or a semicolon should replace the comma after the word "mean" in the quote.

When directly quoting someone, use quotation marks around their words. Periods go inside the closing quotation marks.

Someone is being quoted, and his quote is a question. Therefore, a question mark goes after his question, inside the quotation marks.

A Sentence a Day

Verb form, spelling, commas, run-ons, quotation marks, question marks

incorrect His sister texted him a series of emogee's, happy face, sad face, clown face, sad face, mad face, clown face but he had no idea what that meant.

correct His sister texted him a series of emojis—happy face, sad face, clown face, sad face, mad face, clown face—but he had no idea what that meant.

notes "Emojis" or "emoji" is the correct spelling for more than one "emoji." The *s* is optional.

"Emojis" is not possessive, so no apostrophe is needed.

The list of emojis is a parenthetical aside that interrupts the sentence. Dashes are appropriate to set it off. Parentheses are also acceptable.

Tea was litrally spilled, at Imani's anual tea partie.

Tea was literally spilled at Imani's annual tea party.

Is "tea" being used literally or metaphorically? If tea spilled out of teacups at the tea party, "literally" would be appropriate. If no tea spilled out of teacups at the tea party and "tea" is metaphorically referring to the act of sharing gossip or personal information about someone, the word "literally" is not necessary and could be confusing.

The correct spellings are "literally," "annual," and "party."

The comma between "spilled" and "at" should be deleted.

After Travis posted a U-tube video about the toll increase for any one wishing to cross the bridge; he received hundreds of unhelpful comments from some rather unpleasent Trolls.

After Travis posted a YouTube video about the toll increase for anyone wishing to cross the bridge, he received hundreds of unhelpful comments from some rather unpleasant trolls.

The correct spelling is "anyone" because the sentence is referring to any person wishing to cross the bridge.

A comma is needed after "bridge" because the sentence begins with an introductory clause starting with "after."

"YouTube" and "unpleasant" are the correct spellings.

"Trolls" is a common noun in this sentence, so it is not capitalized. But if you were referring to the movie, *Trolls*, it would be capitalized (and italicized because it is movie title).

incorrect

Why did I read that articull about ear worms, now I have Bohemiam Rapsody stuck in my hed.

correct

Why did I read that article about earworms? Now I have "Bohemian Rhapsody" stuck in my head.

notes

Any sentence that asks a question should have a question mark at the end.

The correct spellings are "article," "earworms," "bohemian," "rhapsody," and "head."

The word "rhapsody" is a common noun and is only capitalized in the example because it is part of the song title. However, the word "bohemian" is a little trickier. It is capitalized in this sentence because it is a part of the song title, but according to the dictionary, it is capitalized when referring to a native or inhabitant of Bohemia and lowercase when it is a noun used to refer to a person living an unconventional life in an artistic way or when it is used as an adjective to refer to anything that reflects a bohemian lifestyle.

This type of run-on sentence is called a comma splice. Two complete sentences cannot be separated by a comma. In this case, a question mark is the best choice because the first clause ("Why did I read that article about earworms") is a question.

Quotation marks go around song titles.

A Sentence a Day

231

Question marks, spelling, capitalization, run-ons, quotation marks

I put on my jetpack, flew to get some fastfood, and bought lunch to-go but I lose halve of my French fries on the way back.

I put on my jet pack, flew to get some fast food, and bought lunch to go, but I lost half of my french fries on the way back.

The correct spellings are "jet pack," "fast food," and "half."

The item above switches from past tense ("flew" and "bought") to present tense ("lose"). The sentence should be rewritten so that all the verbs are in past or present tense. If you're using past tense, "lose" should be "lost." Note that "put" is the same in past or present tense.

There should be a comma before the coordinating conjunction "but."

"To-go" is hyphenated as a compound adjective if it is before the noun it modifies. Because "to go" follows the noun "lunch," it should not be hyphenated.

Capitalization rules can be confusing. Students may wonder why "French" in "french fries" is not capitalized. Actually, both "French fries" and "french fries" are acceptable, but lowercase is preferred by the *Associated Press Stylebook* and the *Chicago Manual of Style*. The argument for lowercase "french" in "french fries" is that "french" refers to the style of cut and not the country. Have students give their reasons for why or why not they would capitalize "French" when referring to fries.

He claimed Chad GPT was his reel name, he had always bean Chad George-Paul Tillsberry.

He claimed Chad G. P. T. was his real name because he had always been Chad George-Paul Tillsberry.

Initials in names need periods and spaces between them: "G. P. T."

The correct spellings are "real" and "been."

This type of run-on sentence is called a comma splice. Two complete sentences cannot be separated by a comma. Use a semicolon, a period, or a conjunction. Some conjunctions don't necessarily require a comma ("because," "if," "though," "since"). Others do require a comma, such as coordinating conjunctions ("for," "and," "nor," "but," "or," "yet," "so," or FANBOYS).

A Sentence a Day

Periods, spelling, run-ons

The magnificient maids will be by your treehouse today at 1:00 p.m. to clean the Living Room Kitchen Bathrooms and Bedrooms, vacuum shampoo and rinse the rugs carpets and curtains, sweep mop and polish the marble floors, in the Arcade, Bowling Alley and Theater, water fertilize and prune the roses venus fly traps and Bonsai trees in the green house and drain refill and disenfect the water in the pool hot tub and lazy river.

The Magnificent Maids will be by your tree house today at 1:00 p.m. to clean the living room, kitchen, and bedrooms; vacuum, shampoo, and rinse the rugs, carpets, and curtains; sweep, mop, and polish the marble floors in the arcade, bowling alley, and theater; water, fertilize, and prune the roses, Venus flytraps, and bonsai trees in the greenhouse; and drain, refill, and disinfect the water in the pool, hot tub, and lazy river.

"Magnificent Maids" is capitalized if it's the name of a cleaning service company. If the maids are magnificent and work for another company, such as Crazy Cleaners, "magnificent maids" would not be capitalized.

The following should not be capitalized because they're common nouns: "living room," "kitchen," "bathrooms," "bedrooms," "arcade," "bowling alley," "theater," and "bonsai."

"Venus" should be capitalized because the Venus flytrap is named after the planet Venus, which is a proper noun.

The correct spellings are "magnificent," "tree house," "flytraps," "greenhouse," and "disinfect."

In this sentence, groups of related items can be separated by semicolons, as demonstrated in the corrected version.

There are several commas missing in this sentence, as the corrected version shows. In long lists with many items, it might be best to use the Oxford comma to keep everything straight.

The comma between "floors" and "in" should be deleted.

A Sentence a Day

Instead of bying an expensive drone she use duck tape to attache her Smart Phone to a remote control helacopter.

Instead of buying an expensive drone, she uses duct tape to attach her smartphone to a remote-controlled helicopter.

The correct spellings are "buying," "attach," "smartphone," and "helicopter."

Whether or not "duck" should be "duct" depends on whether or not the sentence is referring to "duct tape," which is a common noun, or "Duck Tape," which is a brand of duct tape. Note the lowercase "duct tape" and capitalized "Duck Tape."

The word "smartphone" is a common noun, so it should not be capitalized unless it's part of a name.

"Instead of buying an expensive drone" is an introductory phrase. (It comes before the main part of the sentence: "she used duct tape to attach her smartphone to a remote-controlled helicopter.") Therefore, it should be followed by a comma.

The sentence has a singular subject ("she"), so it needs a singular verb—"uses" or "used." "Uses" is present tense, and "used" is past tense, but either one works in this sentence.

Hyphens in compound adjectives signal to the reader that the adjectives ("remote-controlled") all refer to the noun that follows: "helicopter." The dictionary lists "remote control" as the noun and "remote-controlled" as the compound adjective.

A Sentence a Day

Spelling, capitalization, commas, verb form, verb tense, hyphens

Because Tawa was three dimensional printing his 800 feet yacht at the maker space.

Because Tawa was 3D printing his 800-foot yacht at the makerspace, Harper decided to come back next month because it was going to take forever.

The compound adjective "three-dimensional" has a hyphen, but it can be abbreviated as "3D."

"800-foot" is hyphenated because it's a compound adjective modifying "yacht."

The correct word is "foot" when it's used as an adjective.

"Makerspace" can be spelled as one word or two ("maker space").

The item is a sentence fragment. A good follow-up exercise is to have students correct the fragment in at least five different ways, with "because" in the middle of the sentence as well as at the beginning of the sentence.

Because Ramona wore high-heels while rideing her skate-board through a lavuh field she was considered the best skate-boarder of all times.

Because Ramona wore high heels while riding her skateboard through a lava field, she was considered the best skateboarder of all time.

"Because Ramona wore high heels while riding her skateboard through a lava field" is an introductory element (a clause). Therefore, it should be followed by a comma.

The correct spellings are "high heels," "riding," "skateboard," "lava," and "skateboarder."

The phrase is "of all time," not "of all times."

A Sentence a Day

Commas, spelling, word choice

I cant beleive they hasn't invented a App for time travel.

I can't believe they haven't invented an app for time travel.

The correct spellings are "can't" and "believe."

"App" is an abbreviation for "application" and should not be capitalized because it is a common noun.

"They" is plural, so it needs a plural verb—"haven't" or "hadn't."

"A" is used before words beginning with a consonant sound. "An" is used before words beginning with a vowel sound.

Spelling, abbreviations,
capitalization, verb form, word choice

A Sentence a Day

I don't except paranormal explinations accept the ones I here on Pod casts.

I don't accept paranormal explanations except the ones I hear on podcasts.

"Except" means with the exclusion of. "Accept" means to receive or recognize as true.

"Hear" is the word needed, not "here."

The correct spellings are "explanations" and "podcasts."

The word "podcasts" is a common noun, so it should not be capitalized.

A Sentence a Day

Word choice, spelling, capitalization

The computer Virus was not to happy, because it didn't really wanna go virul.

The computer virus was not too happy because it didn't really want to go viral.

There is no reason to capitalize "virus" because it's a common noun.

"Because" is a conjunction that is not generally preceded by a comma. The conjunctions that *are* generally preceded by a comma when they separate two sentences are "for," "and," "nor," "but," "or," and sometimes "yet" and "so" (FANBOYS).

It should be "want to," not "wanna."

"To" should be "too." Although "to" and "too" have several meanings, to keep the basics straight, think "to" as in "to town," "two" as in "count to two," and "too" as in "too much ice cream."

The correct spelling is "viral."

Capitalization, commas, word choice, spelling

A Sentence a Day

Were the seamonsters who live wear the Speed-boaters and
Jetskiers we're forbiddin to go.

We're the sea monsters who live where the speedboaters and
jet skiers were forbidden to go.

"We're" is the word needed at the beginning of the sentence because it is a contraction for "we are."
"Wear" should be "where." Finally, it should be "were forbidden."

The correct spellings are "sea monsters," "speedboaters," "jet skiers," and "forbidden."

Capitalization is not necessary for "speedboaters" because it's a common noun. The term "Jet Skiers"
should be capitalized if the people riding the watercraft are riding jet skis that are trademarked Jet
Skis. If the people are riding any other similar type of watercraft, "jet ski" is lowercase. "Jet ski" is an
example of a trademarked name that has become a common noun. Other examples include "xerox"
and "aspirin." In formal writing, any trademarked name should be capitalized.

A Sentence a Day

Word choice, spelling,
capitalization

The vr head set, was bot by Jayden.

Jayden bought the VR headset.

Active voice means someone or something does something. Passive voice means someone or something has something done to them. Passive voice always uses a "to be" verb (for example, "was" or "were"). For the most part, you want to use active voice in formal writing, but passive voice has its place as well. Usually, you can fix passive voice by putting the subject before the verb and changing the "to be" verb.

Each letter in "VR" is capitalized because it is an acronym for "virtual reality." To be more precise, this example of an acronym is an initialism. An initialism is an acronym where each letter is read as a letter (ATM, DVD) instead of combining the letters into a new word (GIF, BOGO). "VR" cannot really be pronounced in a way that makes sense, so it is an initialism.

The correct spellings are "headset" and "bought."

The comma in the sentence should be deleted, even if the sentence stays in passive voice. There is no need to place a comma between the subject and the verb of a sentence.

The smart fork that started malfunctionining when it wouldn't stop vibrading so intencely that it flue across the counter and ended up with it's tines stuck in dad's special birthday cake that mom ordered from Finland.

The smart fork started malfunctioning when it wouldn't stop vibrating so intensely that it flew across the counter and ended up with its tines stuck in Dad's special birthday cake that Mom ordered from Finland.

Although it is very long, the item above is still a sentence fragment. There is one word in the sentence that could be removed to make it a complete sentence: "that." Or the sentence as is needs to be finished. What *about* the smart fork that started malfunctioning? Try having students complete the sentence in at least two more ways—adding something before the fragment and after the fragment.

The correct spellings are "malfunctioning," vibrating," "intensely," and "flew."

"Dad" and "Mom" are being used as names in this sentence, so they should be capitalized.

"Its" is a pronoun used to show ownership or possession. There is no apostrophe in it.

Fragments, spelling, capitalization, word choice

IYKYK . . . what ever you due, don't reed the coments.

If you know, you know; whatever you do, don't read the comments.

Each letter in "IYKYK" is capitalized because it is an acronym for "If you know, you know." To be more precise, this example of an acronym is an initialism. An initialism is an acronym where each letter is read as a letter (ATM, DVD) instead of combining the letters into a new word (GIF, BOGO). "IYKYK" cannot really be pronounced in a way that makes sense, so it is an initialism.

The rule for acronyms in formal writing when referring to them multiple times is to spell out the words of the acronym the first time you use it and put the capitalized letters for the acronym in parentheses behind the mention. In subsequent referrals, use the capitalized letters for the acronym. This is not necessary for familiar acronyms (FBI, NASA). If you're only referring to the acronym once, spell it out.

An ellipsis has specific uses and should not be substituted for a period. Ellipses indicate when part of a quote is left out, when there's a pause in speech, or when a thought or statement is not completed. The first ellipsis is unnecessary. The sentence can be written with a semicolon, a period, or a conjunction between "know" and "whatever," but the sentence is grammatical without any punctuation or a conjunction between "If you know, you know" and "whatever you do, don't read the comments."

The correct spellings are "whatever," "do," "read," and "comments."

Damari seen that documentry about Hanson Robotics . . . and decides he does'nt need to learn how to cook . . . an ai powerred Robot named Sophia woud do it four him.

Damari saw that documentary about Hanson Robotics and decided he didn't need to learn how to cook; an AI-powered robot named Sophia would do it for him.

The correct verb form here is "saw." "Seen" always needs a helping verb before it—she *has* seen, she *will have* seen, she *was* seen, she *will be* seen, etc.

The correct spellings are "documentary," "doesn't, "powered," "would," and "for."

An ellipsis has specific uses and should not be substituted for a period. Ellipses indicate when part of a quote is left out, when there's a pause in speech, or when a thought or statement is not completed. The first ellipsis is unnecessary. No punctuation is needed after "Robotics." The second ellipsis should be changed to a semicolon, a period, or a conjunction.

The item above switches tenses. It starts out with a verb in past tense ("saw") and switches to present tense ("decides" and "doesn't."). To write the sentence in past tense, change "decides" to "decided," and change "doesn't" to "didn't." To write the sentence in present tense, change "saw" to "sees," leave "decides" and "doesn't" as is, and change "would" to "will."

Hyphens in compound adjectives signal to the reader that the adjectives ("AI-powered") all refer to the noun that follows: "robot."

"AI" is capitalized because it is an acronym for "artificial intelligence." To be more precise, this example of an acronym is an initialism. An initialism is an acronym where each letter is read as a letter (ATM, DVD) instead of combining the letters into a new word (GIF, BOGO). "AI" cannot really be pronounced in a way that makes sense, so it is an initialism.

The rule for acronyms in formal writing when referring to them multiple times is to spell out the words of the acronym the first time you use it and put the capitalized letters for the acronym in parentheses behind the mention. In subsequent referrals, use the capitalized letters for the acronym. This is not necessary for familiar acronyms (FBI, NASA). If you're only referring to the acronym once, spell it out.

There is no reason to capitalize the common noun "robot" unless it's part of a name (the company "iRobot," for example).

A Sentence a Day

Verb form, spelling, ellipses, verb tense, hyphens, acronyms, capitalization

The super hero, insisted on having a pack of wolfs live in his back yard, resulting in affects that effected the intire neighbor hood.

The superhero insisted on having a pack of wolves live in his backyard, resulting in effects that affect the entire neighborhood.

"Affects" is a verb. "Effect" is a noun.

The correct spellings are "superhero," "wolves," "backyard," "entire," and "neighborhood."

The first comma in the sentence should be deleted. There is no need to place a comma between the subject and the verb of a sentence.

Word choice,
spelling, commas

A Sentence a Day

He lay down the baskit of eggs that the chickins laid, called his Boss and lied to her about being sick, then laid on his bed, fell a sleep, and dreamed of egg nog.

He laid down the basket of eggs that the chickens laid, called his boss and lied to her about being sick, then lay on his bed, fell asleep, and dreamed of eggnog.

If you're talking about placing or putting something down, that is "to lay." If you're talking about being horizontal on a surface, such as reclining on a bed, that is "to lie." If you're talking about saying untruthful things, that is "to lie." If you look at a tense chart for these verbs, you will understand why it's so confusing and why so many people have trouble keeping it all straight. You will have to memorize the verb tenses and practice these if you want to be an expert on using "lay" and "lie."

The correct spellings are "basket," "chickens," "asleep," and "eggnog."

The word "boss" is a common noun in this example and should not be capitalized unless it's used as a name ("Hey, Boss, check out these fresh eggs I got for you.")

On the other side of the soler sistem.

The grass is greener on the other side of the solar system.

The item is a sentence fragment. There is no subject or verb.

Try having students complete the sentence in at least two more ways—adding something before the fragment and after the fragment.

The correct spellings are "solar" and "system."

Yesterday was the worse day of my life cause the stupid chat bot don't do a well job of answering my questions.

Yesterday was the worst day of my life because the stupid chatbot didn't do a good job of answering my questions.

"Worst" is the correct word choice here. "Worst" means something is as bad as possible. "Worse" means something is bad in comparison to something else.

"Well" is used to describe how someone *does* something. "Good" is used to describe a noun. Here, the noun "job" is being described, so it should be "good job."

The correct spellings are "because" and "chatbot."

The sentence has a singular subject ("chatbot"), so it needs a singular verb—"doesn't" or "didn't." More than one chatbot would use "don't": "Chatbots don't do a good job."

A Sentence a Day

Word choice, spelling, verb form

Hover Boots are a no brainer, and a win win for every one.

Hover boots are a no-brainer and a win-win for everyone.

Unless "hover boots" is the specific brand name of the boots, it is not capitalized because it's a common noun.

"No-brainer" is a hyphenated compound noun, and "win-win" is a hyphenated compound adjective or noun.

Delete the comma after "no-brainer."

The correct spellings are "no-brainer," "win-win," and "everyone."

Capitalization, hyphens,
commas, spelling

A Sentence a Day

In the novel Servant of the Butterflys the cast-aways on desalation island enjoy a wonderful time together, and have no issues what so ever

In the novel, *Servant of the Butterflies*, the castaways on Desolation Island enjoy a wonderful time together and have no issues whatsoever.

"*Servant of the Butterflies*" is an appositive that interrupts the sentence to give more information about the novel. It should be set off with commas.

Book titles are italicized, so it should be *Servant of the Butterflies*.

The correct spellings are "butterflies," "castaways," "desolation," and "whatsoever."

"Desolation Island" should be capitalized because it is the name of the island.

No comma is needed after "together."

The sentence should end with a period.

A Sentence a Day

Commas, italics, spelling, capitalization, periods

Common Core State Standards Alignment

Grade Level	Common Core State Standards
Grade 5 ELA-Literacy	W.5.5 With guidance and support from peers and adults, develop and strengthen writing as needed by planning, revising, editing, rewriting, or trying a new approach. (Editing for conventions should demonstrate command of Language standards 1–3 up to and including grade 5 here.)
	L.5.1 Demonstrate command of the conventions of standard English grammar and usage when writing or speaking.
	L.5.2 Demonstrate command of the conventions of standard English capitalization, punctuation, and spelling when writing.
	L.5.3 Use knowledge of language and its conventions when writing, speaking, reading, or listening.
Grade 6 ELA-Literacy	W.6.5 With some guidance and support from peers and adults, develop and strengthen writing as needed by planning, revising, editing, rewriting, or trying a new approach. (Editing for conventions should demonstrate command of Language standards 1–3 up to and including grade 6 here.)
	L.6.1 Demonstrate command of the conventions of standard English grammar and usage when writing or speaking.
	L.6.2 Demonstrate command of the conventions of standard English capitalization, punctuation, and spelling when writing.
	L.6.3 Use knowledge of language and its conventions when writing, speaking, reading, or listening.
Grade 7 ELA-Literacy	L.7.1 Demonstrate command of the conventions of standard English grammar and usage when writing or speaking.
	L.7.2 Demonstrate command of the conventions of standard English capitalization, punctuation, and spelling when writing.
Grade 8 ELA-Literacy	L.8.2 Demonstrate command of the conventions of standard English capitalization, punctuation, and spelling when writing.
Grade 9-10 ELA-Literacy	L.9-10.1 Demonstrate command of the conventions of standard English grammar and usage when writing or speaking.
	L.9-10.2 Demonstrate command of the conventions of standard English capitalization, punctuation, and spelling when writing

INDEX

abbreviations 89, 159, 174, 214, 238

acronyms 182, 221, 224, 242, 244–5

active voice 214, 242

apostrophes 14, 23, 28, 31, 49, 51, 64, 72, 89, 91, 111, 114, 121, 126, 137, 139, 154, 156–7, 167, 170, 171–3, 177–8, 186, 191, 201, 205, 221, 223, 228

appositives 5, 115, 176

capitalization 4, 9, 16, 18, 21, 29, 34, 36, 39, 42, 45, 47, 49, 52, 55, 56–7, 60–4, 69–70, 72–4, 76–83, 85, 87–9, 93–6, 98, 100, 102, 111, 116–17, 121, 132, 134, 137, 146–7, 150–1, 153, 157, 159, 161–5, 171, 174, 176–7, 180–2, 184–6, 190, 192, 198–9, 201, 205–7, 210, 212–13, 215, 217, 219–22, 224–6, 230–2, 234–5, 238–41, 243, 245, 247, 250–2

clichés 21, 140, 143, 205

colons 68, 84, 97, 114, 119, 122, 166, 218, 226, 234

commas 1, 3, 5–6, 8–12, 17–18, 21, 25–7, 29, 34–5, 37, 39, 45, 48–9, 52, 57–60, 63, 67, 74–6, 81, 84–6, 88–92, 94–6, 98–9, 101–3, 115, 117–18, 120, 126–8, 131, 134, 138, 149–51, 154, 167, 169, 175–9, 181–6, 188–9, 193–4, 196–7, 199, 201, 204–6, 209–15, 219, 222–3, 226–7, 229–30, 232, 234–5, 237, 240, 242, 246, 250–1

comma splice 19, 23, 30, 33, 44, 49, 78, 88, 94, 99, 104, 108, 111, 113, 152, 156, 160, 170, 174, 180, 199, 201, 217–18, 224–5, 227, 231, 233

conjunctions 19, 21, 23, 30, 33, 44, 70, 78, 87, 104, 108, 111, 113, 120, 152, 160, 170, 173–4, 180, 185, 188, 194, 199, 201, 204, 209, 215, 217–18, 223, 232–3, 240, 244–5

consonant sound 4, 211, 238

contractions 7, 10, 23–4, 31, 33, 34–5, 37, 44, 89, 105, 111, 128–9, 163

coordinating conjunction 19, 23, 30, 33, 44, 78, 87, 108, 111, 113, 120, 152, 160, 170, 173, 180, 185, 188, 194, 199, 201, 204, 215, 217–18, 218, 223, 232, 233

dangling modifiers 107, 110, 145, 147

dashes 75, 102, 175, 228

dependent clause 11, 79, 210

dialogue 13, 18, 69, 74, 134, 178, 191, 193

double negatives 41, 55, 130, 140

double subjects 5, 32, 123, 149, 180, 208

ellipses 82, 244–5

ending element 17

exclamation points 39, 56, 69, 72, 134, 144, 183, 202

FANBOYS 19, 21, 23, 30, 33, 44, 78, 108, 111, 113, 152, 160, 170, 173, 180, 194, 199, 201, 204, 209, 217–18, 223, 233, 240

formal letter 122

formal salutation 122

formal sounding 70

formal writing 5, 214, 221, 224, 241–2, 244–5

fragments 2, 4, 12, 14, 35, 40, 46, 59, 78–9, 82, 105–6, 133, 142, 148, 158, 164–5, 171–2, 187, 195, 236, 243, 248

hyphens 166, 201, 222, 232, 235–6, 245, 250

"i" before "e" rule 1, 3, 31–2, 64, 91, 137, 179, 188, 196

independent clause 40

indirect quote 20

informal conversation 67

informal emails or text messages 48, 63

informally 5, 42

informal speech 65

informal writing 31, 128, 174

introductory element 9, 27, 40, 52, 59–60, 76, 86, 90, 138, 154, 158, 175, 178, 206, 227, 237

introductory phrase 1, 26, 107, 212, 215, 235

italics 132, 153, 204, 251

noun 5, 21, 45, 48, 53, 55, 60, 69, 107, 134, 136, 145, 150–1, 162, 166, 176, 194, 199, 201, 205–7, 210, 212–13, 215, 217, 219–24, 226, 230–2, 234–5, 238–41, 245–7, 249–50

numbers 8, 93, 116, 204, 223

numerals 8, 116, 204

Oxford comma 6, 102, 234

parallelism 113

passive voice 214, 242

period 1, 4, 12, 14, 19, 23, 30, 33, 44, 46, 59, 70, 78, 88, 94, 99, 102, 104, 108, 111, 113, 116, 120, 125, 135, 150, 152, 156, 159–61, 163, 170, 173–4, 180, 199, 201, 217–18, 224, 225, 227, 233, 244–5, 251

plural 25, 82, 104, 136, 152, 223, 238

possession 8, 11, 21, 24, 40, 44, 64, 105, 109, 121, 126, 131, 178, 194, 222, 243

predicate 49

prepositional phrases 25, 60

pronouns 22, 36, 51, 131, 156, 212, 219

punctuation 6, 69, 244–5, 252

question marks 7, 77, 95, 118, 127, 134, 162, 181, 191, 196, 200, 227, 231

quotation marks 18, 20, 35, 39, 42–3, 50, 69, 72–3, 77, 83, 91, 109, 112, 118, 126–7, 130, 132, 144, 151, 153, 168, 181–2, 191–2, 211, 227, 231

run-ons 1, 19, 23, 30, 33, 38, 44, 49, 70, 78, 87–8, 94, 99, 102, 104, 108, 111, 113, 120, 152, 155–6, 160–1, 163, 170, 173–4, 180, 185, 199, 201, 217–8, 224–5, 227, 231

semicolon 1, 19, 23, 30, 33, 44, 70, 78, 88, 94, 99, 104, 108, 111, 113–14, 120, 152, 160, 170, 173–4, 180, 199, 201, 217–18, 224–5, 227, 233, 234, 244–5

serial comma 6, 10, 102

series 6, 10, 48, 59, 74, 84, 98, 102–3, 179, 181–2, 184

singular 131, 136, 235, 249

spelling 1–3, 5–6, 8–9, 11, 15–17, 19–20, 25–7, 29–32, 36–9, 41–2, 44–8, 53–5, 58, 61, 63–6, 68, 70–1, 73, 82, 85, 89–93, 96, 99, 103, 105–6, 108–9, 111–14, 116–17, 123–9, 131–3, 135–40, 144, 148–52, 154–70, 172–4, 176–7, 179, 183–4, 188, 190, 192–7, 199–200, 202–4, 207–12, 214–15, 217–21, 223–52

subject 4, 32, 49, 67, 104, 115, 131, 156, 214, 235, 242, 246, 248–9

subordinate clause 40, 92

tense 104, 112, 119, 125, 140, 160, 196, 206, 223, 232, 235, 243, 245, 247

A Sentence a Day

unnecessary words 54, 65–6, 70, 86, 131, 135–6, 141, 144, 200, 208

verb 4, 12, 24, 48, 62, 67, 80, 82, 84, 95, 104, 112–13, 115, 119, 125, 133, 136, 156, 160, 169, 196–7, 199, 206, 214, 218, 223, 227, 232, 235, 238, 242, 245–9
verb agreement 84, 218
verb forms 24, 62, 95, 104, 113, 136, 156, 227, 235, 238, 245, 249
verb tense 104, 112, 119, 125, 140, 160, 196, 223, 232, 235, 245, 247
vowel sound 4, 8, 14, 45, 60, 111, 176, 211, 238

word choice 3–4, 7–8, 10–11, 13–15, 21–2, 24, 28, 31, 33–5, 40–3, 45, 48, 50, 52–3, 55–6, 60, 62, 65, 67, 71–3, 78, 80–1, 88–90, 92, 94, 97, 100–2, 105–6, 108–9, 111, 115–6, 119, 121–2, 124–5, 127, 129–31, 135, 138–44, 146, 150, 153, 156–7, 159, 161, 165, 170, 174, 176, 178, 187, 189–90, 194–6, 198, 203, 208–9, 213, 216, 220, 222, 229, 236–41, 243, 246–7, 249
words in a series 6, 102